50 Meals on a Boat/Camper Recipes for Home

By: Kelly Johnson

Table of Contents

- Grilled Fish Tacos
- Shrimp Scampi Pasta
- Chicken Kebabs with Vegetables
- Beef Stir-Fry
- Caprese Salad with Balsamic Glaze
- Veggie Quesadillas
- One-Pot Jambalaya
- Spaghetti Carbonara
- Breakfast Burritos
- Lemon Garlic Butter Shrimp
- Campfire Chili
- Grilled Steak with Chimichurri Sauce
- Stuffed Bell Peppers
- Ratatouille
- Baked Salmon with Dill Sauce
- Cauliflower Fried Rice
- BBQ Chicken Sandwiches
- Sweet Potato Hash
- Mediterranean Couscous Salad
- Teriyaki Chicken Skewers
- Black Bean Burgers
- Pad Thai Noodles
- Quinoa Stuffed Peppers
- Grilled Veggie Kabobs
- Tomato Basil Bruschetta
- Campfire Pizza
- Cajun Shrimp Foil Packets
- Chicken Fajita Wraps
- Greek Salad with Grilled Chicken
- Veggie Chili
- Bacon-Wrapped Asparagus
- Stuffed Portobello Mushrooms
- Pesto Pasta Salad
- Grilled Halibut with Lemon Butter Sauce
- Hawaiian BBQ Pork Sliders

- Ratatouille
- Quiche Lorraine
- Teriyaki Beef Skewers
- Coconut Curry Chicken
- Grilled Corn on the Cob
- Stuffed Zucchini Boats
- Mediterranean Stuffed Pitas
- Campfire Nachos
- Chicken and Veggie Foil Packets
- Thai Peanut Noodles
- Grilled Sausage with Peppers and Onions
- Mediterranean Chicken Pita Pockets
- Veggie Spring Rolls
- Campfire Potatoes
- S'mores Dip

Grilled Fish Tacos

Ingredients:

- 1 lb white fish fillets (such as tilapia, cod, or halibut)
- 2 tablespoons olive oil
- 1 teaspoon chili powder
- 1/2 teaspoon ground cumin
- 1/2 teaspoon smoked paprika
- Salt and pepper to taste
- Juice of 1 lime
- 8 small corn or flour tortillas
- 1 cup shredded cabbage or coleslaw mix
- 1/2 cup diced tomatoes
- 1/4 cup chopped fresh cilantro
- Optional toppings: sliced avocado, sour cream, salsa, lime wedges

Instructions:

1. Preheat your grill to medium-high heat.
2. In a small bowl, mix olive oil, chili powder, cumin, smoked paprika, salt, pepper, and lime juice to make a marinade.
3. Pat the fish fillets dry with paper towels. Brush both sides of the fish fillets with the marinade.
4. Grill the fish fillets for about 4-5 minutes per side, or until the fish flakes easily with a fork and is cooked through. Cooking time will depend on the thickness of your fish.
5. While the fish is grilling, warm the tortillas on the grill for about 20-30 seconds per side, until they are lightly charred and pliable.
6. Once the fish is cooked, remove from the grill and let it rest for a minute or two. Then, use a fork to flake the fish into bite-sized pieces.
7. To assemble the tacos, place some shredded cabbage on each tortilla. Top with flaked fish, diced tomatoes, and chopped cilantro. Add any optional toppings as desired.
8. Serve the grilled fish tacos immediately with lime wedges on the side for squeezing over the tacos.

Enjoy your delicious grilled fish tacos while soaking in the scenery on your boat or camper adventure!

Shrimp Scampi Pasta

Ingredients:

- 1 lb shrimp, peeled and deveined
- 8 oz linguine or spaghetti pasta
- 4 tablespoons unsalted butter

- 4 tablespoons olive oil
- 4-5 cloves garlic, minced
- 1/2 teaspoon red pepper flakes (adjust to taste)
- Salt and pepper, to taste
- 1/4 cup dry white wine (optional)
- Juice of 1 lemon
- 1/4 cup chopped fresh parsley
- Grated Parmesan cheese, for serving
- Lemon wedges, for serving

Instructions:

1. Cook the pasta according to package instructions until al dente. Drain and set aside.
2. While the pasta is cooking, prepare the shrimp. Pat them dry with paper towels and season with salt and pepper.
3. In a large skillet, heat 2 tablespoons of butter and 2 tablespoons of olive oil over medium-high heat.
4. Add the minced garlic and red pepper flakes to the skillet. Sauté for about 1 minute, until fragrant.
5. Add the shrimp to the skillet in a single layer. Cook for 2-3 minutes per side, until shrimp are pink and cooked through. Remove the shrimp from the skillet and set aside.
6. If using, pour the white wine into the skillet and let it simmer for 1-2 minutes, scraping up any browned bits from the bottom of the pan.
7. Reduce the heat to medium-low. Add the remaining 2 tablespoons of butter and 2 tablespoons of olive oil to the skillet. Stir until the butter is melted.
8. Return the cooked shrimp to the skillet. Add the cooked pasta, lemon juice, and chopped parsley. Toss everything together until well combined and heated through.
9. Season with additional salt and pepper if needed.
10. Serve the shrimp scampi pasta immediately, garnished with grated Parmesan cheese and lemon wedges on the side.

Enjoy your shrimp scampi pasta while enjoying the views from your boat or camper!

Chicken Kebabs with Vegetables

Ingredients:

- 1 lb chicken breast or thighs, cut into bite-sized pieces
- 1 bell pepper, cut into chunks
- 1 red onion, cut into chunks
- 1 zucchini, sliced
- Cherry tomatoes
- For the marinade:
    - 1/4 cup olive oil
    - Juice of 1 lemon

- 3 cloves garlic, minced
- 1 teaspoon dried oregano
- 1 teaspoon paprika
- Salt and pepper, to taste

Instructions:

1. In a bowl, whisk together all the ingredients for the marinade - olive oil, lemon juice, minced garlic, dried oregano, paprika, salt, and pepper.
2. Place the chicken pieces in a large resealable plastic bag or a bowl. Pour half of the marinade over the chicken, reserving the other half for the vegetables. Seal the bag or cover the bowl, and refrigerate for at least 30 minutes (or up to 4 hours) to marinate.
3. Meanwhile, prepare the vegetables. In a separate bowl, toss the bell pepper chunks, red onion chunks, zucchini slices, and cherry tomatoes with the remaining marinade.
4. Preheat your grill to medium-high heat. If using wooden skewers, soak them in water for at least 30 minutes to prevent them from burning.
5. Thread the marinated chicken, bell pepper, red onion, zucchini, and cherry tomatoes onto skewers, alternating the ingredients.
6. Grill the kebabs for about 10-12 minutes, turning occasionally, until the chicken is cooked through and the vegetables are tender and lightly charred.
7. Remove the kebabs from the grill and let them rest for a few minutes.
8. Serve the chicken kebabs with vegetables immediately, garnished with fresh herbs if desired.

Enjoy these flavorful chicken kebabs with vegetables as a perfect dish for your boat or camper adventure!

Beef Stir-Fry

Ingredients:

- 1 lb beef sirloin or flank steak, thinly sliced
- 2 tablespoons soy sauce
- 1 tablespoon oyster sauce
- 1 tablespoon hoisin sauce
- 1 tablespoon cornstarch
- 1 teaspoon sesame oil
- 2 tablespoons vegetable oil, divided
- 3 cloves garlic, minced
- 1 tablespoon fresh ginger, minced
- 1 onion, thinly sliced
- 1 bell pepper, thinly sliced
- 1 cup broccoli florets
- 1 carrot, thinly sliced
- Salt and pepper, to taste

- Cooked rice or noodles, for serving
- Sesame seeds and chopped green onions, for garnish (optional)

Instructions:

1. In a bowl, combine the soy sauce, oyster sauce, hoisin sauce, cornstarch, and sesame oil. Add the sliced beef and toss to coat. Let it marinate for 15-20 minutes.
2. Heat 1 tablespoon of vegetable oil in a large skillet or wok over medium-high heat.
3. Add the marinated beef to the skillet in a single layer. Cook for 1-2 minutes per side, until browned and cooked through. Remove the beef from the skillet and set aside.
4. In the same skillet, add the remaining tablespoon of vegetable oil. Add the minced garlic and ginger, and sauté for about 30 seconds until fragrant.
5. Add the sliced onion, bell pepper, broccoli florets, and carrot to the skillet. Stir-fry for 3-4 minutes, until the vegetables are tender-crisp.
6. Return the cooked beef to the skillet with the vegetables. Stir everything together and cook for another 1-2 minutes to heat through.
7. Season with salt and pepper to taste.
8. Serve the beef stir-fry hot over cooked rice or noodles.
9. Garnish with sesame seeds and chopped green onions if desired.

Enjoy your delicious beef stir-fry, perfect for a satisfying meal on your boat or camper!

Caprese Salad with Balsamic Glaze

Ingredients:

- Fresh mozzarella cheese, sliced
- Fresh tomatoes, sliced
- Fresh basil leaves
- Balsamic glaze (store-bought or homemade*)
- Extra virgin olive oil
- Salt and pepper, to taste

Instructions:

1. **Prepare the Ingredients:**
   - Slice the fresh mozzarella cheese into rounds.
   - Slice the tomatoes into rounds or wedges, depending on your preference.
   - Pick fresh basil leaves from the stems.
2. **Assemble the Salad:**
   - Arrange the mozzarella slices, tomato slices, and basil leaves on a serving platter or individual plates, alternating them in a pattern.
3. **Drizzle with Olive Oil:**
   - Drizzle extra virgin olive oil over the salad.
4. **Season with Salt and Pepper:**

- Season the salad lightly with salt and pepper, to taste.
5. **Drizzle with Balsamic Glaze:**
    - Generously drizzle balsamic glaze over the salad. The balsamic glaze adds a sweet and tangy flavor that complements the freshness of the ingredients.
6. **Serve:**
    - Serve the Caprese salad immediately as a refreshing appetizer or side dish.
7. **Optional Garnish:**
    - Optionally, garnish with additional fresh basil leaves or a sprinkle of freshly ground black pepper.

*Note: To make homemade balsamic glaze, simmer balsamic vinegar over low heat until it reduces and thickens to a syrupy consistency. Allow it to cool before using.

Enjoy this simple and elegant Caprese salad with balsamic glaze during your outdoor adventures!

Veggie Quesadillas

Ingredients:

- 4 large flour tortillas
- 1 cup shredded cheese (cheddar, Monterey Jack, or a Mexican blend)
- 1 bell pepper, thinly sliced
- 1 small onion, thinly sliced
- 1 cup sliced mushrooms
- 1 cup spinach leaves
- 1 tablespoon olive oil
- Salt and pepper, to taste
- Optional: salsa, sour cream, guacamole for serving

Instructions:

1. **Prepare the Vegetables:**
    - Heat olive oil in a skillet over medium heat. Add sliced bell pepper, onion, and mushrooms. Cook for 5-7 minutes, stirring occasionally, until vegetables are tender. Season with salt and pepper to taste. Remove from heat and set aside.
2. **Assemble the Quesadillas:**
    - Heat a large skillet or griddle over medium heat.
    - Place one tortilla in the skillet. Sprinkle with a layer of shredded cheese.
    - Spread a portion of the sautéed vegetables evenly over half of the tortilla.
    - Add a handful of spinach leaves on top of the vegetables.
    - Sprinkle another layer of cheese over the vegetables and spinach.
    - Fold the empty half of the tortilla over the filling, creating a half-moon shape.
3. **Cook the Quesadillas:**

- Cook the quesadilla for 2-3 minutes on each side, or until golden brown and crispy, and the cheese is melted. Press down gently with a spatula while cooking to help the quesadilla stick together.
4. **Repeat:**
    - Repeat with the remaining tortillas and filling ingredients.
5. **Serve:**
    - Cut each quesadilla into wedges and serve hot.
    - Optionally, serve with salsa, sour cream, or guacamole on the side for dipping.

Enjoy these tasty veggie quesadillas as a satisfying meal during your boat or camper adventure!

One-Pot Jambalaya

Ingredients:

- 1 tablespoon olive oil
- 1 lb chicken breast or thighs, cut into bite-sized pieces
- 1 lb smoked sausage (such as andouille or kielbasa), sliced
- 1 onion, diced
- 1 bell pepper, diced
- 2 celery ribs, diced
- 3 cloves garlic, minced
- 1 can (14.5 oz) diced tomatoes
- 1 cup long-grain white rice
- 2 cups chicken broth
- 1 teaspoon paprika
- 1 teaspoon dried thyme
- 1 teaspoon dried oregano
- 1/2 teaspoon cayenne pepper (adjust to taste)
- Salt and pepper, to taste
- 1 lb shrimp, peeled and deveined
- Chopped green onions, for garnish
- Hot sauce, for serving (optional)

Instructions:

1. **Heat Olive Oil:**
    - In a large pot or Dutch oven, heat olive oil over medium-high heat.
2. **Cook Chicken and Sausage:**
    - Add chicken pieces and sausage slices to the pot. Cook for 5-6 minutes, stirring occasionally, until chicken is browned on all sides and sausage is lightly browned. Remove chicken and sausage from the pot and set aside.
3. **Sauté Vegetables:**
    - Add diced onion, bell pepper, celery, and minced garlic to the pot. Sauté for 4-5 minutes, until vegetables are softened.

4. **Add Tomatoes and Rice:**
   - Stir in diced tomatoes (with juices) and rice. Cook for 1-2 minutes, stirring occasionally.
5. **Add Broth and Spices:**
   - Pour in chicken broth and add paprika, dried thyme, dried oregano, cayenne pepper, salt, and pepper. Stir well to combine.
6. **Simmer:**
   - Bring the mixture to a boil. Reduce heat to low, cover, and simmer for 15-20 minutes, or until rice is tender and most of the liquid is absorbed.
7. **Add Shrimp:**
   - Stir in the peeled and deveined shrimp. Cover and cook for an additional 5 minutes, or until shrimp are pink and cooked through.
8. **Finish and Serve:**
   - Once shrimp are cooked, return the cooked chicken and sausage to the pot. Stir well to combine and heat through.
   - Taste and adjust seasoning if needed.
   - Garnish with chopped green onions.
   - Serve hot, optionally with hot sauce on the side for those who prefer an extra kick.

Enjoy this delicious and satisfying one-pot jambalaya as a complete meal during your outdoor adventures!

Spaghetti Carbonara

Ingredients:

- 12 oz spaghetti
- 4 oz pancetta or bacon, diced
- 3 large eggs
- 1 cup grated Pecorino Romano cheese (or Parmesan), plus extra for serving
- Freshly ground black pepper, to taste
- Salt, to taste
- Optional: chopped fresh parsley for garnish

Instructions:

1. **Cook the Pasta:**
   - Bring a large pot of salted water to a boil. Cook the spaghetti according to package instructions until al dente. Reserve 1 cup of pasta cooking water, then drain the spaghetti.
2. **Prepare the Sauce:**
   - While the pasta is cooking, heat a large skillet over medium heat. Add the diced pancetta or bacon and cook until crispy, about 5-7 minutes. Remove from heat and set aside.

3. **Whisk Eggs and Cheese:**
    - In a bowl, whisk together the eggs, grated Pecorino Romano cheese, and a generous amount of freshly ground black pepper.
4. **Combine Pasta and Sauce:**
    - Immediately after draining the pasta, add it to the skillet with the crispy pancetta or bacon. Toss well to combine and heat the pasta slightly.
5. **Add Egg Mixture:**
    - Remove the skillet from heat (important to prevent scrambling the eggs). Quickly pour the egg and cheese mixture over the hot pasta, tossing continuously to coat the pasta evenly. The heat from the pasta will cook the eggs to create a creamy sauce. If the sauce seems too thick, gradually add some of the reserved pasta cooking water until desired consistency is reached.
6. **Serve:**
    - Season with salt to taste (if needed, pancetta or bacon and Pecorino Romano cheese are already salty). Garnish with additional grated cheese, freshly ground black pepper, and chopped fresh parsley, if desired.
7. **Enjoy:**
    - Serve immediately while hot, ensuring each serving is creamy and flavorful.

This spaghetti carbonara recipe is simple yet delicious, making it a perfect choice for a satisfying meal on a boat or camper adventure!

Breakfast Burritos

Ingredients:

- 6 large flour tortillas
- 6 large eggs
- 1/4 cup milk
- 1 cup shredded cheddar cheese (or your favorite cheese)
- 6 slices bacon, cooked and chopped (or sausage, if preferred)
- 1 cup diced bell peppers (any color)
- 1/2 cup diced onion
- Salt and pepper, to taste
- Optional toppings: salsa, sour cream, avocado slices, chopped fresh cilantro

Instructions:

1. Prepare the Eggs:
    - In a bowl, whisk together the eggs and milk. Season with salt and pepper.
2. Cook the Eggs:
    - Heat a large skillet over medium heat. Add a drizzle of oil or a pat of butter if needed. Pour in the egg mixture and scramble until fully cooked. Remove from heat and set aside.
3. Prepare the Fillings:

- In the same skillet (or a separate one), cook the bacon until crispy. Remove and chop into pieces. Alternatively, cook sausage until browned. Remove excess fat, leaving about 1 tablespoon in the skillet.
- Add diced bell peppers and onions to the skillet. Sauté for 3-4 minutes until softened.

4. Assemble the Burritos:
    - Warm the flour tortillas in a microwave or a dry skillet for a few seconds to make them pliable.
    - Divide the scrambled eggs, shredded cheese, cooked bacon or sausage, and sautéed bell peppers and onions evenly among the tortillas, placing the fillings in the center of each tortilla.
5. Fold the Burritos:
    - Fold in the sides of each tortilla, then roll it up tightly from the bottom to enclose the fillings.
6. Serve or Store:
    - Serve the breakfast burritos immediately, or wrap each burrito individually in foil for later. They can be stored in the refrigerator for a few days or frozen for longer storage.
7. Optional:
    - Serve with salsa, sour cream, avocado slices, or chopped fresh cilantro on the side for additional flavor.

Enjoy these delicious and satisfying breakfast burritos as a convenient meal during your boat or camper adventure!

Lemon Garlic Butter Shrimp

Ingredients:

- 1 lb large shrimp, peeled and deveined
- 4 tablespoons unsalted butter
- 4 cloves garlic, minced
- Zest of 1 lemon
- Juice of 1 lemon
- 1/4 teaspoon red pepper flakes (optional, for a bit of heat)
- Salt and pepper, to taste
- Fresh parsley, chopped (for garnish)
- Cooked rice or pasta, for serving

Instructions:

1. Prepare the Shrimp:
    - Pat the shrimp dry with paper towels. Season with salt and pepper.
2. Cook the Shrimp:
    - In a large skillet, melt 2 tablespoons of butter over medium-high heat.
    - Add the shrimp in a single layer and cook for 2-3 minutes per side, until pink and opaque. Remove shrimp from the skillet and set aside.
3. Make the Lemon Garlic Butter Sauce:
    - In the same skillet, melt the remaining 2 tablespoons of butter over medium heat.
    - Add minced garlic and red pepper flakes (if using). Sauté for about 1 minute until garlic is fragrant, being careful not to burn it.
    - Stir in lemon zest and lemon juice. Cook for another minute to combine flavors.
4. Combine and Serve:
    - Return the cooked shrimp to the skillet. Toss well to coat the shrimp evenly with the lemon garlic butter sauce.
    - Cook for an additional minute to heat the shrimp through.
    - Taste and adjust seasoning with salt and pepper if needed.
5. Garnish and Serve:
    - Remove from heat and garnish with chopped fresh parsley.
    - Serve the lemon garlic butter shrimp immediately over cooked rice or pasta.

Enjoy this delicious lemon garlic butter shrimp as a delightful and quick meal during your boat or camper adventure!

Campfire Chili

Ingredients:

- 1 lb ground beef or turkey
- 1 onion, diced
- 2 cloves garlic, minced
- 1 bell pepper, diced
- 1 can (14.5 oz) diced tomatoes
- 1 can (15 oz) kidney beans, drained and rinsed
- 1 can (15 oz) black beans, drained and rinsed
- 1 can (6 oz) tomato paste
- 2 cups beef or vegetable broth
- 1 tablespoon chili powder
- 1 teaspoon ground cumin
- 1/2 teaspoon smoked paprika
- Salt and pepper, to taste
- Optional toppings: shredded cheese, sour cream, chopped green onions, jalapeños, cornbread

Instructions:

1. Prepare the Campfire:
    - If cooking over a campfire, set up a grill grate or a sturdy pot stand over the fire. You'll need a pot or Dutch oven that can withstand the heat.
2. Cook the Ground Meat:
    - Heat a large pot or Dutch oven over medium-high heat. Add the ground beef or turkey and cook until browned, breaking it up with a spoon as it cooks.
3. Add Vegetables:
    - Add diced onion, minced garlic, and diced bell pepper to the pot. Cook for 3-4 minutes, until vegetables are softened.
4. Combine Ingredients:
    - Stir in diced tomatoes (with juices), kidney beans, black beans, tomato paste, and beef or vegetable broth.
5. Seasonings:
    - Add chili powder, ground cumin, smoked paprika, salt, and pepper. Stir well to combine.
6. Simmer:
    - Bring the chili to a boil, then reduce the heat to low. Cover the pot and let it simmer for at least 30 minutes to allow the flavors to meld together. Stir occasionally.
7. Adjust Consistency:
    - If the chili becomes too thick, add more broth or water as needed.
8. Serve:

- - Serve the campfire chili hot, topped with shredded cheese, sour cream, chopped green onions, or any other desired toppings.
  - Enjoy with cornbread or crusty bread on the side.

This campfire chili is a comforting meal that's easy to prepare and perfect for enjoying outdoors during your boat or camper adventure! Adjust the heat level by adding more or less chili powder and enjoy the rich flavors of this hearty dish.

Grilled Steak with Chimichurri Sauce

Ingredients:

For the Steak:

- 2 lbs steak (such as ribeye, sirloin, or flank steak)
- Salt and pepper, to taste
- Olive oil, for brushing

For the Chimichurri Sauce:

- 1 cup fresh parsley, finely chopped
- 1/4 cup fresh cilantro, finely chopped
- 4 cloves garlic, minced
- 1/4 cup red wine vinegar
- 1/2 cup extra virgin olive oil
- 1 tablespoon fresh oregano, chopped (or 1 teaspoon dried oregano)
- 1/2 teaspoon red pepper flakes (optional)
- Salt and pepper, to taste

Instructions:

1. Prepare the Chimichurri Sauce:
    - In a bowl, combine the finely chopped parsley, cilantro, minced garlic, red wine vinegar, olive oil, chopped oregano, and red pepper flakes (if using). Stir well to combine.
    - Season with salt and pepper to taste. Set aside to let the flavors meld while you prepare the steak.
2. Prepare the Steak:
    - Preheat your grill to medium-high heat. If using a boat or camper grill, ensure it's properly preheated and cleaned.
    - Season the steak generously with salt and pepper on both sides. Brush lightly with olive oil to prevent sticking on the grill.
3. Grill the Steak:
    - Place the steak on the preheated grill. Grill for about 4-5 minutes per side for medium-rare, or adjust cooking time according to your desired doneness (about 5-6 minutes for medium, or longer for well-done).
    - Use tongs to flip the steak only once during cooking. Avoid pressing down on the steak with a spatula, as this releases juices and can cause flare-ups.
4. Rest the Steak:
    - Once cooked to your liking, remove the steak from the grill and let it rest for 5-10 minutes on a cutting board. This allows the juices to redistribute throughout the meat.
5. Slice and Serve:

- Slice the steak against the grain into thin slices. Arrange the slices on a serving platter.
- Drizzle the chimichurri sauce generously over the grilled steak slices, or serve the sauce on the side for dipping.

6. Enjoy:
    - Serve the grilled steak with chimichurri sauce immediately, accompanied by your favorite sides like grilled vegetables, potatoes, or a fresh salad.

Grilled steak with chimichurri sauce is a delightful dish that combines the smoky flavor of the steak with the vibrant and tangy flavors of the chimichurri sauce. It's sure to be a hit during your boat or camper adventure!

Stuffed Bell Peppers

Ingredients:

- 4 large bell peppers, any color
- 1 lb ground beef or turkey
- 1 cup cooked rice (white or brown)
- 1 small onion, finely chopped
- 2 cloves garlic, minced
- 1 can (14.5 oz) diced tomatoes, drained
- 1 cup shredded cheese (such as cheddar or Monterey Jack)
- 1 teaspoon dried oregano
- 1 teaspoon dried basil
- Salt and pepper, to taste
- Optional: chopped fresh parsley or basil for garnish

Instructions:

1. Prepare the Bell Peppers:
    - Preheat your oven to 375°F (190°C).
    - Cut the tops off the bell peppers and remove the seeds and membranes from inside. Rinse the peppers under cold water.
2. Cook the Filling:
    - In a large skillet, cook the ground beef or turkey over medium-high heat until browned, breaking it up with a spoon as it cooks.
    - Add chopped onion and minced garlic to the skillet. Cook for 2-3 minutes until onion is softened.
3. Combine Ingredients:
    - Stir in cooked rice, diced tomatoes, dried oregano, dried basil, salt, and pepper. Cook for another 2-3 minutes, allowing flavors to blend together.
4. Stuff the Bell Peppers:
    - Place the hollowed-out bell peppers upright in a baking dish. Spoon the filling mixture evenly into each pepper until they are full.
5. Bake the Stuffed Peppers:
    - Cover the baking dish with foil and bake in the preheated oven for 30-35 minutes, or until the peppers are tender.
6. Add Cheese (Optional):
    - Remove the foil from the baking dish. Sprinkle shredded cheese over the tops of the stuffed peppers.
    - Return the peppers to the oven and bake uncovered for an additional 5-10 minutes, or until the cheese is melted and bubbly.
7. Serve:
    - Remove the stuffed bell peppers from the oven. Garnish with chopped fresh parsley or basil, if desired.

- Serve hot as a complete meal or with a side salad.

Enjoy these delicious stuffed bell peppers as a wholesome and flavorful dish during your boat or camper adventure!

Ratatouille

Ingredients:

- 1 eggplant, diced
- 2 zucchinis, diced
- 1 bell pepper, diced (any color)
- 1 onion, diced
- 2 cloves garlic, minced
- 3 tomatoes, diced
- 2 tablespoons tomato paste
- 1 teaspoon dried thyme
- 1 teaspoon dried oregano
- Salt and pepper, to taste
- Olive oil, for cooking
- Fresh basil leaves, chopped (optional, for garnish)

Instructions:

1. Prepare the Vegetables:
    - Dice the eggplant, zucchinis, bell pepper, onion, and tomatoes into evenly sized pieces.
2. Sauté the Vegetables:
    - Heat a large skillet or pot over medium heat. Add a drizzle of olive oil.
    - Add the diced onion and minced garlic. Sauté for 2-3 minutes until softened and fragrant.
3. Add Eggplant and Bell Pepper:
    - Add the diced eggplant and bell pepper to the skillet. Cook for another 5-7 minutes, stirring occasionally, until they start to soften.
4. Add Zucchini and Tomatoes:
    - Add the diced zucchinis and tomatoes to the skillet. Stir well to combine.
5. Season and Simmer:
    - Stir in the tomato paste, dried thyme, dried oregano, salt, and pepper. Mix until everything is evenly coated.
    - Reduce the heat to low, cover the skillet or pot, and let the ratatouille simmer for 20-25 minutes, stirring occasionally, until all the vegetables are tender and flavors have melded together.
6. Adjust Seasoning:
    - Taste and adjust seasoning with salt and pepper if needed.
7. Serve:
    - Remove from heat and let the ratatouille rest for a few minutes.
    - Serve hot, garnished with chopped fresh basil leaves if desired.
8. Optional Serving Suggestions:

- Ratatouille can be enjoyed on its own as a vegetarian main dish, or served alongside crusty bread, rice, quinoa, or pasta.
- It also pairs well with grilled meat or fish if you're looking to add protein to the meal.

Ratatouille is a comforting and flavorful dish that's perfect for using up summer vegetables and enjoying during your boat or camper adventure. Bon appétit!

Baked Salmon with Dill Sauce

Ingredients:

- 4 salmon fillets, skin-on or skinless (about 6 oz each)
- Salt and pepper, to taste
- 1 tablespoon olive oil
- 1/2 cup sour cream or Greek yogurt
- 2 tablespoons mayonnaise
- 1 tablespoon Dijon mustard
- 2 tablespoons chopped fresh dill (or 2 teaspoons dried dill)
- Zest and juice of 1 lemon
- 1 clove garlic, minced (optional)
- 1/4 teaspoon salt, or to taste
- Fresh dill sprigs, for garnish (optional)

Instructions:

1. Preheat the Oven:
    - Preheat your oven to 400°F (200°C). Line a baking sheet with parchment paper or foil for easy cleanup.
2. Prepare the Salmon:
    - Pat the salmon fillets dry with paper towels. Season both sides with salt and pepper.
    - Place the salmon fillets on the prepared baking sheet. Drizzle with olive oil and rub to coat evenly.
3. Bake the Salmon:
    - Bake the salmon in the preheated oven for 12-15 minutes, depending on the thickness of the fillets, or until the salmon is cooked through and flakes easily with a fork.
4. Make the Dill Sauce:
    - While the salmon is baking, prepare the dill sauce. In a small bowl, combine sour cream (or Greek yogurt), mayonnaise, Dijon mustard, chopped fresh dill, lemon zest, lemon juice, minced garlic (if using), and salt. Mix well until smooth and creamy.
5. Serve:
    - Once the salmon is done baking, remove it from the oven.
    - Serve the baked salmon hot, topped with a generous spoonful of dill sauce.
    - Garnish with fresh dill sprigs, if desired.

Tips:

- Variations: You can add a touch of honey or maple syrup to the dill sauce for a hint of sweetness.

- Side Suggestions: Baked salmon with dill sauce pairs well with steamed vegetables, roasted potatoes, or a fresh green salad.
- Storage: Store any leftover dill sauce in an airtight container in the refrigerator for up to 3 days. It also makes a great dip for veggies or a sauce for grilled chicken.

This baked salmon with dill sauce recipe is perfect for a family dinner or a special occasion. The creamy dill sauce complements the tender salmon beautifully, creating a dish that's both elegant and comforting. Enjoy the delightful flavors of fresh dill, lemon, and savory salmon!

Cauliflower Fried Rice

Ingredients:

- 1 medium head of cauliflower (about 4 cups of cauliflower rice)
- 2 tablespoons sesame oil (or vegetable oil)
- 2 cloves garlic, minced
- 1 small onion, finely chopped
- 1 cup frozen peas and carrots mix (thawed)
- 2 eggs, beaten
- 3 tablespoons soy sauce (or tamari for gluten-free)
- 1 tablespoon oyster sauce (optional)
- 1 teaspoon grated fresh ginger (optional)
- Salt and pepper, to taste
- 2 green onions, thinly sliced (for garnish)
- Sesame seeds, for garnish (optional)

Instructions:

1. Prepare the Cauliflower Rice:
    - Cut the cauliflower into florets and discard the core. Place the florets in a food processor and pulse until they resemble rice grains. You may need to do this in batches.
2. Cook the Cauliflower Rice:
    - Heat 1 tablespoon of sesame oil (or vegetable oil) in a large skillet or wok over medium heat.
    - Add minced garlic and chopped onion. Cook for 2-3 minutes until softened and fragrant.
3. Add Vegetables and Eggs:
    - Stir in the thawed peas and carrots mix. Cook for another 2 minutes until heated through.
    - Push the vegetables to one side of the skillet and pour the beaten eggs into the other side. Allow the eggs to cook undisturbed for a few seconds until they begin to set. Then, scramble the eggs with a spatula until cooked through.
4. Combine Everything:
    - Add the cauliflower rice to the skillet with the cooked vegetables and eggs. Stir well to combine.
5. Season the Fried Rice:
    - Drizzle the remaining tablespoon of sesame oil over the cauliflower rice.
    - Add soy sauce (or tamari), oyster sauce (if using), and grated ginger (if using). Stir everything together until well combined.
6. Finish and Serve:

- Cook for another 3-4 minutes, stirring occasionally, until the cauliflower rice is tender but still has a slight crunch. Taste and adjust seasoning with salt and pepper if needed.
7. **Garnish and Serve:**
    - Remove the skillet from heat. Garnish the cauliflower fried rice with sliced green onions and sesame seeds, if desired.
    - Serve hot as a main dish or as a side dish with your favorite protein.

Tips:

- Protein Options: Add cooked chicken, shrimp, tofu, or diced ham for extra protein.
- Variations: Customize with additional vegetables like bell peppers, broccoli, or mushrooms.
- Storage: Cauliflower fried rice can be stored in an airtight container in the refrigerator for up to 3 days. Reheat gently in a skillet or microwave before serving.

Enjoy this cauliflower fried rice as a nutritious and satisfying meal that's packed with flavor and vegetables, perfect for a quick weeknight dinner or meal prep!

BBQ Chicken Sandwiches

Ingredients:

- 2 boneless, skinless chicken breasts (about 1 lb)
- Salt and pepper, to taste
- 1 cup barbecue sauce (your favorite variety)
- 4 sandwich buns (hamburger buns or ciabatta rolls work well)
- 1 tablespoon olive oil or vegetable oil
- Optional toppings: sliced red onion, coleslaw, pickles, cheese slices

Instructions:

1. Prepare the Chicken:
    - Season the chicken breasts with salt and pepper on both sides.
2. Cook the Chicken:
    - Option 1: Grill the chicken breasts over medium-high heat for 5-6 minutes per side, or until fully cooked (internal temperature reaches 165°F or 74°C).
    - Option 2: Heat olive oil or vegetable oil in a large skillet over medium heat. Cook the chicken breasts for 6-7 minutes per side, or until cooked through.
3. Shred or Slice the Chicken:
    - Once cooked, transfer the chicken to a cutting board and let it rest for a few minutes. Then, shred the chicken using two forks or slice it thinly against the grain.
4. Coat with BBQ Sauce:
    - In a bowl, toss the shredded or sliced chicken with barbecue sauce until evenly coated. Adjust the amount of sauce to your liking.
5. Assemble the Sandwiches:
    - Toast the sandwich buns lightly, if desired.
    - Divide the BBQ chicken mixture evenly among the bottom halves of the sandwich buns.
6. Add Toppings (Optional):
    - Add sliced red onion, coleslaw, pickles, cheese slices, or any other toppings you prefer.
7. Serve:
    - Place the top halves of the sandwich buns over the BBQ chicken.
    - Serve immediately and enjoy your BBQ chicken sandwiches!

Tips:

- Variations: Experiment with different barbecue sauces, such as sweet, spicy, or smoky varieties, to change the flavor profile of your sandwiches.
- Side Suggestions: Serve BBQ chicken sandwiches with potato chips, fries, or a side salad for a complete meal.

- Make-Ahead: The shredded BBQ chicken can be prepared ahead of time and stored in the refrigerator for up to 3 days. Reheat gently before assembling sandwiches.

This recipe is perfect for a quick and satisfying meal, ideal for lunch or dinner. BBQ chicken sandwiches are versatile and can be customized to suit your taste preferences, making them a family favorite!

Sweet Potato Hash

Ingredients:

- 2 medium sweet potatoes, peeled and diced into small cubes
- 1 tablespoon olive oil or butter
- 1 small onion, diced
- 1 bell pepper, diced (any color)
- 2 cloves garlic, minced
- 1 teaspoon smoked paprika (or regular paprika)
- 1/2 teaspoon ground cumin
- Salt and pepper, to taste
- Optional: chopped fresh parsley or cilantro for garnish
- Optional add-ins: cooked bacon or sausage, spinach, kale, or diced tomatoes

Instructions:

1. Prepare the Sweet Potatoes:
    - Peel the sweet potatoes and dice them into small, uniform cubes.
2. Cook the Sweet Potatoes:
    - Heat olive oil or butter in a large skillet over medium heat.
    - Add the diced sweet potatoes to the skillet and spread them out in an even layer.
    - Cook for about 10-12 minutes, stirring occasionally, until the sweet potatoes are tender and lightly browned. Adjust the heat as needed to prevent burning.
3. Add Vegetables:
    - Push the sweet potatoes to one side of the skillet and add diced onion and bell pepper to the empty side.
    - Cook for 3-4 minutes, stirring occasionally, until the vegetables are softened.
4. Season the Hash:
    - Stir in minced garlic, smoked paprika, ground cumin, salt, and pepper. Cook for 1-2 minutes until the spices are fragrant.
5. Optional Add-Ins:
    - If using any optional add-ins like cooked bacon or sausage, spinach, kale, or diced tomatoes, add them to the skillet now and cook until heated through.
6. Finish and Serve:
    - Remove the skillet from heat.
    - Taste and adjust seasoning if needed.
    - Garnish with chopped fresh parsley or cilantro, if desired.
    - Serve the sweet potato hash hot as a side dish or a main course, optionally topped with a fried or poached egg for a complete meal.

Tips:

- Texture: For crispier sweet potatoes, cook them longer without stirring too frequently.

- Variations: Customize your sweet potato hash with your favorite vegetables and spices.
- Storage: Leftover sweet potato hash can be stored in an airtight container in the refrigerator for up to 3 days. Reheat gently in a skillet or microwave before serving.

This sweet potato hash recipe is versatile, nutritious, and perfect for breakfast, brunch, or even as a side dish for dinner. Enjoy the delicious combination of sweet and savory flavors in every bite!

Mediterranean Couscous Salad

Ingredients:

- 1 cup couscous (instant or traditional)
- 1 1/4 cups vegetable or chicken broth (or water)
- 1/4 cup extra virgin olive oil
- 2 tablespoons lemon juice (about 1 lemon)
- 1 clove garlic, minced
- 1 teaspoon Dijon mustard
- 1/2 teaspoon honey (optional, to taste)
- Salt and pepper, to taste
- 1 cucumber, diced
- 1 pint cherry tomatoes, halved
- 1/2 red bell pepper, diced
- 1/2 yellow bell pepper, diced
- 1/4 cup red onion, finely chopped
- 1/4 cup Kalamata olives, pitted and chopped
- 1/4 cup fresh parsley, chopped
- 1/4 cup fresh mint, chopped
- 1/4 cup crumbled feta cheese (optional)
- Optional: 1/4 cup chopped roasted red peppers, artichoke hearts, or chickpeas for added flavor and texture

Instructions:

1. Cook the Couscous:
    - In a medium saucepan, bring the vegetable or chicken broth (or water) to a boil.
    - Stir in the couscous, cover, and remove from heat. Let it sit for 5 minutes, then fluff with a fork to separate the grains. Transfer the couscous to a large mixing bowl and let it cool.
2. Prepare the Dressing:
    - In a small bowl, whisk together the extra virgin olive oil, lemon juice, minced garlic, Dijon mustard, honey (if using), salt, and pepper until well combined.
3. Assemble the Salad:
    - Add the diced cucumber, halved cherry tomatoes, diced bell peppers, finely chopped red onion, chopped Kalamata olives, fresh parsley, and fresh mint to the bowl with the cooled couscous.
    - Pour the dressing over the salad ingredients in the bowl. Toss gently to combine until everything is evenly coated with the dressing.
4. Optional Add-Ins:
    - If desired, add chopped roasted red peppers, artichoke hearts, or chickpeas for additional flavor and texture.
5. Chill and Serve:

- Cover the bowl and refrigerate the Mediterranean couscous salad for at least 30 minutes to allow the flavors to meld together.
- Before serving, taste and adjust seasoning if needed. Sprinkle crumbled feta cheese over the top, if using, and gently toss again.

6. Serve:
    - Serve the Mediterranean couscous salad chilled or at room temperature.
    - Garnish with additional fresh herbs or a drizzle of olive oil, if desired.

Tips:

- Make-Ahead: This salad can be made ahead of time and stored in the refrigerator for up to 2 days. Add the fresh herbs and feta cheese just before serving for best results.
- Variations: Customize the salad with your favorite Mediterranean ingredients like sun-dried tomatoes, pine nuts, or grilled vegetables.
- Gluten-Free Option: Use quinoa instead of couscous for a gluten-free version of this salad.

This Mediterranean couscous salad is perfect as a light lunch, side dish, or as part of a buffet spread. It's full of fresh flavors and textures that will surely delight your taste buds!

Teriyaki Chicken Skewers

Ingredients:

- 1 lb boneless, skinless chicken thighs or chicken breast, cut into 1-inch cubes
- Wooden skewers, soaked in water for at least 30 minutes (or use metal skewers)
- 1/4 cup soy sauce (or tamari for gluten-free)
- 2 tablespoons honey or brown sugar
- 2 tablespoons rice vinegar
- 1 tablespoon sesame oil
- 2 cloves garlic, minced
- 1 teaspoon grated fresh ginger
- 1/4 teaspoon red pepper flakes (optional, for a bit of heat)
- 2 tablespoons water
- Sesame seeds, for garnish (optional)
- Sliced green onions, for garnish (optional)

Instructions:

1. Prepare the Marinade:
   - In a bowl, whisk together soy sauce (or tamari), honey (or brown sugar), rice vinegar, sesame oil, minced garlic, grated ginger, red pepper flakes (if using), and water until well combined.
2. Marinate the Chicken:
   - Place the chicken cubes in a shallow dish or resealable plastic bag. Pour half of the teriyaki marinade over the chicken, reserving the other half for later. Make sure the chicken is evenly coated. Marinate in the refrigerator for at least 30 minutes, or up to 2 hours.
3. Preheat the Grill (or Oven):
   - Preheat your grill to medium-high heat. Alternatively, you can use a grill pan on the stove or preheat your oven broiler.
4. Skewer the Chicken:
   - Thread the marinated chicken cubes onto the soaked wooden skewers, leaving a little space between each piece.
5. Grill the Skewers:
   - Place the skewers on the preheated grill (or grill pan) and cook for 5-6 minutes per side, or until the chicken is fully cooked through and has nice grill marks. Baste the skewers with the reserved teriyaki marinade while grilling.
6. Serve:
   - Once cooked through, remove the teriyaki chicken skewers from the grill.
   - Sprinkle with sesame seeds and sliced green onions, if desired, for garnish.
   - Serve hot with rice or noodles, and steamed vegetables.

Tips:

- Chicken: Chicken thighs are preferred for their juiciness, but you can use chicken breast if you prefer.
- Sauce: Boil the leftover marinade for a few minutes to use as a dipping sauce if desired.
- Variations: Add diced pineapple, bell peppers, or onions between the chicken pieces on the skewers for added flavor and color.

These teriyaki chicken skewers are perfect for a barbecue, picnic, or weeknight dinner. They're easy to make and packed with delicious Asian-inspired flavors that everyone will love!

Black Bean Burgers

Ingredients:

- 1 can (15 oz) black beans, drained and rinsed
- 1/2 cup breadcrumbs (regular or gluten-free)
- 1/4 cup finely chopped onion
- 1/4 cup finely chopped bell pepper (any color)
- 1 clove garlic, minced
- 1 teaspoon ground cumin
- 1 teaspoon chili powder
- 1/2 teaspoon smoked paprika (optional)
- 1/4 teaspoon cayenne pepper (optional, for heat)
- Salt and pepper, to taste
- 1 tablespoon soy sauce (or tamari for gluten-free)
- 1 tablespoon olive oil
- 1 egg (or flax egg for vegan option)
- Burger buns
- Optional toppings: lettuce, tomato slices, avocado slices, cheese, mayo, mustard, ketchup

Instructions:

1. Prepare the Black Bean Mixture:
   - In a large mixing bowl, mash the black beans with a fork or potato masher until mostly smooth, leaving some chunks for texture.
2. Add Ingredients:
   - Add breadcrumbs, finely chopped onion, bell pepper, minced garlic, ground cumin, chili powder, smoked paprika (if using), cayenne pepper (if using), salt, pepper, soy sauce, olive oil, and egg (or flax egg) to the bowl with the mashed black beans.
3. Mix and Form Patties:
   - Mix everything together until well combined. If the mixture feels too wet, add a bit more breadcrumbs. If it's too dry, add a splash of water or additional olive oil.
   - Divide the mixture into 4 equal portions and shape each portion into a patty, about 1/2 to 3/4 inch thick. Place the patties on a plate or baking sheet lined with parchment paper.
4. Cook the Burgers:
   - Heat a skillet or grill pan over medium heat. Add a drizzle of olive oil to coat the pan.
   - Cook the black bean burgers for 4-5 minutes per side, or until they are heated through and have a golden-brown crust on the outside. You can also grill the burgers over medium-high heat for about the same amount of time per side.
5. Assemble the Burgers:

- Toast the burger buns lightly if desired.
- Place each black bean patty on a bun.
- Add your favorite toppings such as lettuce, tomato slices, avocado slices, cheese, mayo, mustard, or ketchup.

6. **Serve:**
   - Serve the black bean burgers immediately while warm.
   - Enjoy these flavorful and nutritious burgers!

Tips:

- **Make-Ahead:** You can prepare the black bean mixture in advance and refrigerate it for up to 24 hours before cooking.
- **Freezing:** You can freeze uncooked black bean patties. Place parchment paper between each patty to prevent sticking, then store them in a freezer-safe container for up to 3 months. Thaw before cooking.
- **Vegan Option:** Use a flax egg (1 tablespoon ground flaxseed meal + 3 tablespoons water, let sit for 5 minutes to thicken) instead of a regular egg.

These homemade black bean burgers are a fantastic vegetarian or vegan alternative to traditional burgers. They're satisfying, flavorful, and versatile—perfect for a quick weeknight dinner or weekend barbecue!

Pad Thai Noodles

Ingredients:

- 8 oz (about 225g) flat rice noodles (pad Thai noodles)
- 2 tablespoons tamarind paste
- 3 tablespoons fish sauce (or soy sauce for vegetarian/vegan)
- 2 tablespoons brown sugar (or palm sugar)
- 1 tablespoon rice vinegar
- 1/2 teaspoon chili flakes, or more to taste
- 2 tablespoons vegetable oil
- 1 block of firm tofu, cut into small cubes (optional)
- 2 cloves garlic, minced
- 1 shallot, thinly sliced
- 2 eggs, lightly beaten
- 1 cup bean sprouts
- 4 green onions, sliced (white and green parts separated)
- 1/4 cup roasted peanuts, chopped
- Lime wedges, for serving
- Fresh cilantro, for garnish (optional)

Instructions:

1. Prepare the Rice Noodles:
    - Cook the rice noodles according to the package instructions until they are tender but still slightly firm (al dente). Drain and rinse with cold water to stop the cooking process. Set aside.
2. Make the Pad Thai Sauce:
    - In a small bowl, whisk together tamarind paste, fish sauce (or soy sauce), brown sugar, rice vinegar, and chili flakes until well combined. Adjust the sweetness and saltiness to your taste by adding more sugar or fish sauce if needed.
3. Cook the Tofu (if using):
    - Heat 1 tablespoon of vegetable oil in a large skillet or wok over medium-high heat. Add the cubed tofu and cook until golden brown on all sides, about 5-7 minutes. Remove from the skillet and set aside.
4. Stir-Fry the Aromatics:
    - In the same skillet or wok, heat the remaining tablespoon of vegetable oil over medium heat. Add minced garlic and sliced shallot, and sauté for 1-2 minutes until fragrant and softened.
5. Cook the Eggs:
    - Push the garlic and shallot to the side of the skillet, creating a space in the center. Pour the lightly beaten eggs into the center and let them cook undisturbed for a few seconds until they start to set. Scramble the eggs with a spatula until fully cooked and then mix them with the garlic and shallot.

6. Combine Everything:
    - Add the cooked rice noodles and prepared Pad Thai sauce to the skillet. Toss everything together until the noodles are well coated with the sauce.
7. Add Vegetables and Tofu:
    - Stir in bean sprouts, sliced green onions (white parts), and cooked tofu (if using). Cook for another 2-3 minutes, stirring occasionally, until heated through.
8. Serve:
    - Remove the skillet from heat. Taste and adjust seasoning if needed by adding more fish sauce, sugar, or chili flakes.
    - Serve Pad Thai noodles hot, garnished with chopped roasted peanuts, sliced green onions (green parts), lime wedges, and fresh cilantro (if using).

Tips:

- Variations: Customize your Pad Thai noodles by adding shrimp, chicken, or more vegetables like bell peppers and carrots.
- Tamarind Paste Substitute: If you can't find tamarind paste, you can use lime juice as a substitute, though the flavor will be slightly different.
- Spice Level: Adjust the amount of chili flakes to suit your spice preference.

Enjoy this homemade Pad Thai noodles recipe as a delicious and satisfying meal that brings the flavors of Thailand to your table!

Quinoa Stuffed Peppers

Ingredients:

- 4 large bell peppers (any color)
- 1 cup quinoa, rinsed
- 2 cups vegetable broth or water
- 1 tablespoon olive oil
- 1 small onion, finely chopped
- 2 cloves garlic, minced
- 1 medium zucchini, diced
- 1 medium carrot, diced
- 1 cup diced tomatoes (fresh or canned)
- 1 teaspoon ground cumin
- 1 teaspoon paprika
- Salt and pepper, to taste
- 1/2 cup grated cheese (such as cheddar or mozzarella), optional
- Fresh herbs (such as parsley or cilantro), for garnish

Instructions:

1. Prepare the Quinoa:
    - In a medium saucepan, bring the vegetable broth or water to a boil. Add the rinsed quinoa, reduce heat to low, cover, and simmer for 15-20 minutes, or until the quinoa is cooked and the liquid is absorbed. Remove from heat and let it sit, covered, for 5 minutes. Fluff with a fork and set aside.
2. Prepare the Bell Peppers:
    - Preheat your oven to 375°F (190°C). Cut the tops off the bell peppers and remove the seeds and membranes. If necessary, trim the bottoms slightly to help them stand upright in a baking dish.
3. Cook the Filling:
    - Heat olive oil in a large skillet over medium heat. Add chopped onion and cook for 3-4 minutes until softened.
    - Add minced garlic, diced zucchini, and diced carrot to the skillet. Cook for another 5-6 minutes until the vegetables are tender.
    - Stir in diced tomatoes, ground cumin, paprika, salt, and pepper. Cook for 2-3 minutes more, allowing the flavors to blend together.
4. Combine Quinoa and Vegetables:
    - Add the cooked quinoa to the skillet with the vegetables. Stir well to combine and cook for another 2-3 minutes. Taste and adjust seasoning if needed.
5. Stuff the Peppers:
    - Spoon the quinoa and vegetable mixture evenly into the hollowed-out bell peppers. Press gently to pack the filling.
6. Bake the Stuffed Peppers:

- Place the stuffed peppers upright in a baking dish. If desired, sprinkle grated cheese on top of each pepper.
- Cover the dish with foil and bake in the preheated oven for 30-35 minutes, or until the peppers are tender and the filling is heated through.

7. Serve:
   - Remove the stuffed peppers from the oven. Garnish with fresh herbs, such as parsley or cilantro, if desired.
   - Serve hot as a main dish or a hearty side dish.

Tips:

- **Variations:** Feel free to customize the filling with your favorite vegetables or add cooked protein like ground turkey, chicken, or beans.
- **Make-Ahead:** You can prepare the quinoa and vegetable filling ahead of time and store it in an airtight container in the refrigerator for up to 2 days before assembling and baking the stuffed peppers.
- **Vegan Option:** Omit the cheese or use a dairy-free cheese alternative to make this dish vegan-friendly.

These quinoa stuffed peppers are not only delicious and satisfying but also packed with protein and nutrients. They make a fantastic meal for a family dinner or a healthy option for meal prep!

Grilled Veggie Kabobs

Ingredients:

- Assorted vegetables, such as:
    - Cherry tomatoes
    - Bell peppers (any color), cut into chunks
    - Zucchini, sliced into rounds
    - Red onion, cut into wedges
    - Mushrooms, whole or halved
    - Eggplant, cut into chunks
- Olive oil, for brushing
- Salt and pepper, to taste
- Optional: herbs (such as rosemary or thyme), garlic powder, lemon zest

Instructions:

1. Prepare the Vegetables:
    - Wash and cut the vegetables into bite-sized pieces, ensuring they are all roughly the same size for even cooking.
2. Assemble the Kabobs:
    - If using wooden skewers, soak them in water for at least 30 minutes to prevent them from burning on the grill.
    - Thread the vegetables onto the skewers, alternating colors and types of vegetables for an attractive presentation.
3. Season the Kabobs:
    - Brush the assembled kabobs with olive oil and sprinkle with salt, pepper, and any optional seasonings or herbs of your choice.
4. Preheat the Grill:
    - Preheat your grill to medium-high heat. Make sure the grates are clean and lightly oiled to prevent sticking.
5. Grill the Kabobs:
    - Place the vegetable kabobs on the preheated grill. Cook for about 10-12 minutes, turning occasionally, until the vegetables are tender and lightly charred.
6. Serve:
    - Remove the grilled veggie kabobs from the grill and transfer them to a serving platter.
    - Optional: Drizzle with a little more olive oil or a squeeze of fresh lemon juice before serving.

Tips:

- Marinade or Sauce: You can marinate the vegetables before threading them onto skewers for extra flavor. Use a simple marinade of olive oil, garlic, herbs, and lemon juice.
- Grilling Variations: If using smaller vegetables like cherry tomatoes or mushrooms, you can grill them in a grill basket or skewer them separately.
- Presentation: Serve the grilled veggie kabobs as a side dish, appetizer, or as a main course with rice or salad.

Grilled veggie kabobs are not only delicious but also healthy and versatile. They are perfect for summer grilling, outdoor gatherings, or anytime you want to enjoy fresh and flavorful vegetables with a smoky twist!

Tomato Basil Bruschetta

Ingredients:

- 4-5 ripe tomatoes, diced
- 1/4 cup fresh basil leaves, chopped (plus extra for garnish)
- 2 cloves garlic, minced
- 1 tablespoon balsamic vinegar
- 2 tablespoons extra virgin olive oil
- Salt and pepper, to taste
- 1 French baguette or Italian loaf, sliced
- Olive oil, for brushing

Instructions:

1. Prepare the Tomato Basil Mixture:
    - In a medium bowl, combine the diced tomatoes, chopped fresh basil, minced garlic, balsamic vinegar, extra virgin olive oil, salt, and pepper. Mix well to combine all the ingredients. Taste and adjust seasoning if needed. Set aside to marinate for at least 15-20 minutes to allow the flavors to meld together.
2. Prepare the Bread:
    - Preheat the oven to 375°F (190°C).
    - Slice the baguette or Italian loaf into 1/2-inch thick slices. Place the slices on a baking sheet in a single layer.
3. Toast the Bread:
    - Lightly brush both sides of each bread slice with olive oil.
    - Toast the bread slices in the preheated oven for about 8-10 minutes, or until they are golden brown and crisp on the edges. Alternatively, you can grill the bread slices on a grill pan or outdoor grill for a smoky flavor.
4. Assemble the Bruschetta:
    - Once the bread slices are toasted, spoon a generous amount of the tomato basil mixture onto each slice.
5. Serve:
    - Arrange the tomato basil bruschetta slices on a serving platter.
    - Garnish with additional chopped basil leaves on top for a fresh finish.

Tips:

- Variations: Add a sprinkle of grated Parmesan cheese or a drizzle of balsamic glaze over the bruschetta for extra flavor.
- Make-Ahead: You can prepare the tomato basil mixture ahead of time and store it in the refrigerator. Toast the bread slices just before serving to keep them crisp.
- Customization: Adjust the amount of garlic, basil, and vinegar to suit your taste preferences.

Tomato basil bruschetta is perfect as an appetizer for parties or as a light snack. It's simple to prepare yet incredibly flavorful, making it a favorite among both guests and hosts alike!

Campfire Pizza

Ingredients:

- Pizza dough (store-bought or homemade)
- Olive oil, for brushing
- Pizza sauce (store-bought or homemade)
- Shredded mozzarella cheese
- Your favorite pizza toppings (e.g., pepperoni, bell peppers, mushrooms, onions, olives, etc.)
- Optional: Fresh basil leaves, grated Parmesan cheese, red pepper flakes

Instructions:

1. Prepare the Campfire:
    - Build a campfire and let it burn down until you have hot coals. You'll want a medium-high heat for cooking the pizza.
2. Prepare the Pizza Dough:
    - If using store-bought pizza dough, follow the package instructions for any necessary resting or rising time.
    - If making homemade dough, prepare it ahead of time and divide it into individual portions suitable for personal-sized pizzas.
3. Roll Out the Dough:
    - On a lightly floured surface, roll out each portion of pizza dough into a circle or rectangle, about 1/4 inch thick.
4. Preheat the Cast Iron Skillet:
    - Place a cast iron skillet or grill grate over the campfire and let it preheat for a few minutes until hot. Brush the skillet with olive oil to prevent sticking.
5. Cook the Pizza Dough:
    - Carefully transfer one piece of rolled-out dough to the hot skillet. Cook for 1-2 minutes on each side, or until the dough puffs up slightly and starts to develop grill marks. Remove from skillet and set aside.
6. Assemble the Pizza:
    - Spread a thin layer of pizza sauce over the cooked side of the dough.
    - Sprinkle shredded mozzarella cheese over the sauce, then add your favorite toppings.
7. Cook the Pizza:
    - Carefully place the topped pizza back into the hot skillet (uncooked side down) or directly onto the grill grate.
    - Cover with a lid or foil and cook for 5-7 minutes, or until the cheese is melted and bubbly, and the bottom of the pizza crust is golden brown.
8. Serve:
    - Remove the campfire pizza from the skillet or grill and transfer to a cutting board.

- - Sprinkle with fresh basil leaves, grated Parmesan cheese, and red pepper flakes if desired.
  - Slice and serve hot.

Tips:

- Variations: Experiment with different toppings and sauces to customize your campfire pizza.
- Heat Management: Adjust the heat of your campfire to ensure the pizza cooks evenly without burning.
- Cleanup: Cast iron skillets are durable and easy to clean, but make sure to properly care for them after use.

Enjoy the rustic charm and delicious flavors of campfire pizza outdoors, perfect for camping trips, backyard gatherings, or any outdoor adventure!

Cajun Shrimp Foil Packets

Ingredients:

- 1 lb large shrimp, peeled and deveined
- 1 andouille sausage, sliced into rounds (optional)
- 1 bell pepper, thinly sliced
- 1 red onion, thinly sliced
- 2 cloves garlic, minced
- 1 tablespoon Cajun seasoning
- 1 teaspoon paprika
- 1/2 teaspoon dried thyme
- 1/2 teaspoon dried oregano
- Salt and pepper, to taste
- 2 tablespoons olive oil
- Fresh parsley, chopped (for garnish)
- Lemon wedges (for serving)

Instructions:

1. Preheat the Grill or Oven:
    - Preheat your grill to medium-high heat, or preheat your oven to 400°F (200°C).
2. Prepare the Foil Packets:
    - Cut four large pieces of heavy-duty aluminum foil, about 12x12 inches each.
    - Place equal portions of shrimp, andouille sausage (if using), bell pepper slices, and red onion slices in the center of each piece of foil.
3. Season the Ingredients:
    - In a small bowl, mix together Cajun seasoning, paprika, dried thyme, dried oregano, minced garlic, salt, and pepper.
    - Drizzle olive oil over the shrimp and vegetables in each foil packet. Sprinkle the Cajun seasoning mixture evenly over each packet.
4. Seal the Foil Packets:
    - Fold the sides of the foil over the shrimp and vegetable mixture, then fold up the ends to create sealed packets. Make sure to leave a little room for heat circulation inside the packets.
5. Grill or Bake the Foil Packets:
    - Place the foil packets directly on the grill grates or on a baking sheet in the oven.
    - Grill for 10-12 minutes, or bake in the oven for 15-18 minutes, until the shrimp are pink and opaque, and the vegetables are tender.
6. Serve:
    - Carefully open the foil packets (watch out for steam) and transfer the contents to serving plates or bowls.
    - Garnish with chopped fresh parsley and serve with lemon wedges on the side for squeezing over the shrimp.

Tips:

- Variations: You can customize these Cajun shrimp foil packets by adding other vegetables like corn, cherry tomatoes, or asparagus.
- Spice Level: Adjust the amount of Cajun seasoning and paprika to suit your taste preferences.
- Serve with: Cajun shrimp foil packets are delicious served over rice, quinoa, or with crusty bread to soak up the flavorful juices.

Enjoy these Cajun shrimp foil packets for a flavorful and hassle-free meal that's perfect for outdoor gatherings or a quick weeknight dinner!

Chicken Fajita Wraps

Ingredients:

- 1 lb chicken breasts, thinly sliced
- 1 red bell pepper, thinly sliced
- 1 green bell pepper, thinly sliced
- 1 yellow or orange bell pepper, thinly sliced
- 1 onion, thinly sliced
- 2 tablespoons fajita seasoning (store-bought or homemade)
- 2 tablespoons olive oil
- Salt and pepper, to taste
- 6-8 large flour tortillas (burrito size)
- Optional toppings: shredded cheese, sour cream, salsa, guacamole, shredded lettuce, diced tomatoes

Instructions:

1. Prepare the Chicken and Vegetables:
   - In a bowl, toss the sliced chicken with the fajita seasoning, salt, and pepper until well coated.
   - Heat 1 tablespoon of olive oil in a large skillet over medium-high heat. Add the seasoned chicken and cook until browned and cooked through, about 5-6 minutes per side. Remove the chicken from the skillet and set aside.
2. Cook the Peppers and Onions:
   - In the same skillet, add the remaining tablespoon of olive oil. Add the sliced bell peppers and onion. Cook, stirring occasionally, until the vegetables are tender and slightly caramelized, about 5-6 minutes. Season with salt and pepper to taste.
3. Assemble the Fajita Wraps:
   - Warm the flour tortillas in the microwave for a few seconds or in a dry skillet for about 15-20 seconds per side until soft and pliable.
   - Spoon some of the cooked chicken and sautéed peppers and onions onto each tortilla.
4. Add Toppings:
   - Add your favorite toppings to each wrap, such as shredded cheese, sour cream, salsa, guacamole, shredded lettuce, and diced tomatoes.
5. Roll Up the Wraps:
   - Fold the sides of the tortilla over the filling, then roll it up tightly from the bottom to enclose the filling.
6. Serve:
   - Serve the chicken fajita wraps immediately, whole or sliced in half diagonally for easier handling.

Tips:

- Make-Ahead: You can prepare the chicken and sautéed vegetables ahead of time and store them in the refrigerator. Warm them up before assembling the wraps.
- Variations: Use steak, shrimp, or tofu instead of chicken for different protein options. You can also add additional vegetables like mushrooms or zucchini.
- Grilled Option: For extra flavor, grill the chicken and vegetables instead of cooking them in a skillet.

These chicken fajita wraps are perfect for a quick and flavorful meal that the whole family will enjoy. They're versatile and can be customized with your favorite toppings and extras!

Greek Salad with Grilled Chicken

Ingredients:

For the Grilled Chicken:

- 1 lb chicken breasts, boneless and skinless
- 2 tablespoons olive oil
- Juice of 1 lemon
- 2 cloves garlic, minced
- 1 teaspoon dried oregano
- Salt and pepper, to taste

For the Greek Salad:

- 1 large cucumber, diced
- 1 pint cherry tomatoes, halved
- 1 red bell pepper, diced
- 1/2 red onion, thinly sliced
- 1/2 cup Kalamata olives, pitted
- 1/2 cup crumbled feta cheese
- Fresh parsley or oregano, chopped (for garnish)
- Optional: 1/4 cup sliced pepperoncini peppers

For the Greek Vinaigrette:

- 1/4 cup extra virgin olive oil
- 2 tablespoons red wine vinegar
- 1 tablespoon lemon juice
- 1 teaspoon Dijon mustard
- 1 clove garlic, minced
- 1 teaspoon dried oregano
- Salt and pepper, to taste

Instructions:

1. Marinate and Grill the Chicken:
    - In a bowl, whisk together olive oil, lemon juice, minced garlic, dried oregano, salt, and pepper. Place the chicken breasts in a resealable plastic bag or shallow dish and pour the marinade over them. Seal or cover and refrigerate for at least 30 minutes, or up to 4 hours.
    - Preheat the grill to medium-high heat. Grill the chicken breasts for 6-7 minutes per side, or until cooked through and no longer pink in the center. Remove from the grill and let rest for a few minutes before slicing.
2. Prepare the Greek Salad:

- In a large bowl, combine diced cucumber, cherry tomatoes, diced bell pepper, thinly sliced red onion, Kalamata olives, crumbled feta cheese, and sliced pepperoncini peppers (if using).
3. Make the Greek Vinaigrette:
    - In a small bowl, whisk together extra virgin olive oil, red wine vinegar, lemon juice, Dijon mustard, minced garlic, dried oregano, salt, and pepper until well combined.
4. Assemble the Salad:
    - Pour the Greek vinaigrette over the salad ingredients in the bowl. Toss gently to coat everything evenly with the dressing.
5. Serve:
    - Divide the Greek salad among serving plates or bowls.
    - Slice the grilled chicken breasts and arrange them on top of each salad portion.
    - Garnish with chopped fresh parsley or oregano.

Tips:

- Variations: Add sliced avocado, roasted red peppers, or artichoke hearts to the salad for extra flavor and texture.
- Make-Ahead: You can grill the chicken and prepare the salad ingredients and vinaigrette ahead of time. Keep them separate and assemble just before serving.
- Vegetarian Option: Skip the grilled chicken and serve the Greek salad with chickpeas or grilled tofu for a vegetarian version.

This Greek salad with grilled chicken is perfect for a healthy lunch or light dinner, combining vibrant flavors and textures that will transport you to the Mediterranean!

Veggie Chili

Ingredients:

- 2 tablespoons olive oil
- 1 large onion, diced
- 3 cloves garlic, minced
- 1 red bell pepper, diced
- 1 green bell pepper, diced
- 2 medium carrots, diced
- 1 zucchini, diced
- 1 yellow squash, diced
- 1 jalapeño, seeded and minced (optional, for heat)
- 2 tablespoons chili powder
- 1 tablespoon ground cumin
- 1 teaspoon smoked paprika
- 1 teaspoon dried oregano
- 1/2 teaspoon cayenne pepper (adjust to taste)
- Salt and pepper, to taste
- 1 (28 oz) can crushed tomatoes
- 1 (15 oz) can black beans, drained and rinsed
- 1 (15 oz) can kidney beans, drained and rinsed
- 1 (15 oz) can corn kernels, drained (or use frozen corn)
- 2 cups vegetable broth
- 1 tablespoon tomato paste
- Juice of 1 lime
- Fresh cilantro, chopped (for garnish)
- Optional toppings: shredded cheese, sour cream, avocado slices, chopped green onions

Instructions:

1. Sauté Vegetables:
    - Heat olive oil in a large pot or Dutch oven over medium heat. Add diced onion and sauté for 3-4 minutes until softened.
    - Add minced garlic, diced bell peppers, carrots, zucchini, yellow squash, and jalapeño (if using). Cook for another 5-6 minutes until vegetables begin to soften.
2. Add Spices:
    - Stir in chili powder, cumin, smoked paprika, dried oregano, cayenne pepper, salt, and pepper. Cook for 1-2 minutes until fragrant.
3. Combine Remaining Ingredients:
    - Add crushed tomatoes, black beans, kidney beans, corn kernels, vegetable broth, and tomato paste to the pot. Stir well to combine.
4. Simmer:

- Bring the chili to a boil, then reduce heat to low. Let it simmer uncovered for 20-25 minutes, stirring occasionally, until the vegetables are tender and the flavors have melded together.
5. Finish and Serve:
    - Stir in fresh lime juice. Taste and adjust seasoning if needed.
    - Serve hot, garnished with chopped fresh cilantro and your choice of optional toppings.

Tips:

- Variations: Add other vegetables like mushrooms, sweet potatoes, or bell peppers to suit your taste.
- Texture: For a thicker chili, mash some of the beans or vegetables with a fork before simmering.
- Storage: Veggie chili tastes even better the next day as the flavors continue to develop. Store leftovers in an airtight container in the refrigerator for up to 4 days or freeze for longer storage.

This veggie chili is not only delicious and nutritious but also versatile and customizable. It's a perfect meatless option that everyone will enjoy, whether they're vegetarian or not!

Bacon-Wrapped Asparagus

Ingredients:

- 1 lb (about 450g) asparagus spears, woody ends trimmed
- 10-12 slices of bacon (thin-cut works best)
- Olive oil, for drizzling
- Salt and pepper, to taste
- Optional: Garlic powder, grated Parmesan cheese, lemon wedges for serving

Instructions:

1. Preheat the Oven:
   - Preheat your oven to 400°F (200°C). Line a baking sheet with parchment paper or aluminum foil for easy cleanup.
2. Prepare the Asparagus:
   - Wash the asparagus spears and trim off the tough ends (usually about 1-2 inches from the bottom).
3. Wrap with Bacon:
   - Take one slice of bacon and wrap it around one asparagus spear, starting from the bottom and spiraling upwards. Place the bacon-wrapped asparagus on the prepared baking sheet. Repeat with the remaining asparagus and bacon slices.
4. Season:
   - Drizzle the bacon-wrapped asparagus with a little olive oil. Season lightly with salt and pepper. If desired, sprinkle with a pinch of garlic powder for extra flavor.
5. Bake:
   - Bake in the preheated oven for 20-25 minutes, or until the bacon is crispy and the asparagus is tender. You may need to flip the asparagus halfway through baking to ensure even cooking.
6. Serve:
   - Remove from the oven and transfer the bacon-wrapped asparagus to a serving platter. Optionally, sprinkle with grated Parmesan cheese while still warm.
   - Serve hot with lemon wedges on the side for squeezing over the asparagus.

Tips:

- Variations: For a twist, you can sprinkle the bacon-wrapped asparagus with brown sugar before baking for a sweet and savory flavor.
- Grilling Option: You can also grill the bacon-wrapped asparagus over medium-high heat for 8-10 minutes, turning occasionally, until the bacon is crispy and the asparagus is tender.
- Presentation: Arrange the bacon-wrapped asparagus neatly on a platter for a beautiful appetizer presentation.

Bacon-wrapped asparagus is a crowd-pleasing dish that's perfect for parties, holidays, or even a special weeknight dinner. It combines the crispiness of bacon with the freshness of asparagus, making it a delightful combination of flavors and textures.

Stuffed Portobello Mushrooms

Ingredients:

- 4 large portobello mushrooms
- 2 tablespoons olive oil
- 2 cloves garlic, minced
- 1 small onion, finely chopped
- 1/2 cup breadcrumbs (plain or seasoned)
- 1/2 cup grated Parmesan cheese
- 1/4 cup chopped fresh parsley
- Salt and pepper, to taste
- Optional: 1/4 cup chopped sun-dried tomatoes, 1/4 cup chopped spinach, 1/4 cup chopped bell peppers
- Additional grated Parmesan cheese or breadcrumbs for topping

Instructions:

1. Prepare the Portobello Mushrooms:
    - Preheat your oven to 400°F (200°C). Line a baking sheet with parchment paper.
    - Clean the portobello mushrooms by wiping them gently with a damp paper towel to remove any dirt. Remove the stems by twisting them off, and use a spoon to scrape out the gills (the dark underside of the mushroom caps). Be careful not to break the mushroom caps.
2. Prepare the Filling:
    - In a skillet, heat olive oil over medium heat. Add minced garlic and chopped onion, and sauté until the onion is translucent and garlic is fragrant, about 3-4 minutes.
    - Remove from heat and stir in breadcrumbs, grated Parmesan cheese, chopped parsley, and any optional ingredients like sun-dried tomatoes, spinach, or bell peppers. Season with salt and pepper to taste.
3. Stuff the Mushrooms:
    - Place the portobello mushrooms on the prepared baking sheet, gill side up. Divide the filling mixture evenly among the mushroom caps, pressing gently to pack the filling.
4. Bake:
    - Bake in the preheated oven for 20-25 minutes, or until the mushrooms are tender and the filling is golden brown on top.
5. Serve:
    - Remove from the oven and let cool slightly before serving.
    - Optionally, sprinkle with additional grated Parmesan cheese or breadcrumbs before serving.

Tips:

- Variations: Experiment with different fillings such as chopped nuts, cooked quinoa or rice, or different cheeses like feta or goat cheese.
- Grilling Option: You can also grill stuffed portobello mushrooms over medium-high heat for about 10-15 minutes, or until the mushrooms are tender and the filling is heated through.
- Serve as a Main Dish: Pair stuffed portobello mushrooms with a side salad or roasted vegetables for a satisfying vegetarian main course.

Stuffed portobello mushrooms are versatile and can be customized to suit your taste preferences. They are perfect for entertaining or as a special meal at home, offering a rich and savory dish that's sure to impress!

Pesto Pasta Salad

Ingredients:

- 12 oz (340g) pasta (such as fusilli, penne, or rotini)
- 1/2 cup basil pesto (homemade or store-bought)
- 1 cup cherry tomatoes, halved
- 1/2 cup Kalamata olives, sliced
- 1/2 cup roasted red peppers, chopped
- 1/4 cup red onion, thinly sliced
- 1/4 cup pine nuts, toasted (optional)
- Salt and pepper, to taste
- Fresh basil leaves, chopped (for garnish)
- Grated Parmesan cheese (optional)

Instructions:

1. Cook the Pasta:
   - Cook the pasta according to package instructions in a large pot of salted boiling water until al dente. Drain and rinse under cold water to stop the cooking process. Let it cool slightly.
2. Prepare the Ingredients:
   - In a large bowl, combine the cooked and cooled pasta with cherry tomatoes, Kalamata olives, roasted red peppers, red onion, and pine nuts (if using).
3. Add Pesto:
   - Add basil pesto to the pasta and toss gently to coat everything evenly. Adjust the amount of pesto according to your preference. If the pasta salad seems dry, you can add a little extra olive oil or a splash of pasta cooking water.
4. Season:
   - Season with salt and pepper to taste. Remember that the pesto and olives are already salty, so taste before adding additional salt.
5. Chill and Serve:
   - Cover the bowl with plastic wrap and refrigerate for at least 1 hour to allow the flavors to meld together.
   - Before serving, garnish with chopped fresh basil leaves and grated Parmesan cheese if desired.

Tips:

- Variations: You can add other ingredients to the pesto pasta salad such as grilled chicken, artichoke hearts, sun-dried tomatoes, or fresh mozzarella pearls.
- Make-Ahead: Pesto pasta salad can be made ahead of time and stored in the refrigerator for up to 2 days. Keep it covered to prevent it from drying out.
- Serve Cold: Serve the pasta salad chilled or at room temperature for best flavor.

This pesto pasta salad is vibrant and full of fresh flavors from the basil pesto and assorted vegetables. It's a versatile dish that pairs well with grilled meats, seafood, or as a standalone vegetarian option. Enjoy this delicious and easy-to-make pasta salad for your next gathering!

Grilled Halibut with Lemon Butter Sauce

Ingredients:

For the Grilled Halibut:

- 4 halibut fillets, about 6 oz each, skin removed
- 2 tablespoons olive oil
- Salt and pepper, to taste
- Lemon wedges, for serving

For the Lemon Butter Sauce:

- 1/4 cup unsalted butter
- 2 cloves garlic, minced
- Zest of 1 lemon
- Juice of 1 lemon
- 1 tablespoon chopped fresh parsley
- Salt and pepper, to taste

Instructions:

1. Prepare the Halibut:
    - Preheat your grill to medium-high heat (about 400°F / 200°C).
    - Pat dry the halibut fillets with paper towels. Brush both sides of each fillet with olive oil, then season generously with salt and pepper.
2. Grill the Halibut:
    - Place the halibut fillets directly on the grill grates. Grill for about 4-5 minutes per side, depending on the thickness of the fillets, until the fish is opaque and easily flakes with a fork. Avoid overcooking to keep the halibut moist and tender.
3. Make the Lemon Butter Sauce:
    - While the halibut is grilling, prepare the lemon butter sauce. In a small saucepan, melt the butter over medium heat.
    - Add minced garlic to the melted butter and sauté for about 1 minute until fragrant.
    - Stir in lemon zest, lemon juice, and chopped parsley. Season with salt and pepper to taste. Remove from heat and set aside.
4. Serve:
    - Transfer the grilled halibut fillets to serving plates or a platter.
    - Spoon the lemon butter sauce over the halibut fillets just before serving.
    - Garnish with additional chopped parsley and serve with lemon wedges on the side for squeezing over the fish.

Tips:

- Grilling Tips: Ensure your grill grates are clean and well-oiled before grilling to prevent sticking. Use a fish spatula to carefully flip the halibut fillets to avoid breaking them.
- Variations: You can add a pinch of red pepper flakes to the lemon butter sauce for a touch of heat, or incorporate capers for extra flavor.
- Serving Suggestions: Grilled halibut with lemon butter sauce pairs well with steamed vegetables, rice pilaf, or a fresh salad.

Enjoy this grilled halibut with lemon butter sauce for a delicious and elegant seafood dish that's perfect for a special dinner or entertaining guests!

Hawaiian BBQ Pork Sliders

Ingredients:

For the Hawaiian BBQ Pork:

- 2 lbs pork shoulder or pork butt, trimmed of excess fat
- Salt and pepper, to taste
- 1 cup Hawaiian BBQ sauce (store-bought or homemade, see below)
- 1 cup pineapple juice
- 1/2 cup low-sodium chicken broth
- 1 onion, thinly sliced
- 3 cloves garlic, minced
- Slider buns, for serving

For the Homemade Hawaiian BBQ Sauce:

- 1 cup ketchup
- 1/4 cup low-sodium soy sauce
- 1/4 cup brown sugar
- 1/4 cup pineapple juice
- 2 tablespoons apple cider vinegar
- 1 tablespoon Worcestershire sauce
- 1 teaspoon garlic powder
- 1 teaspoon ground ginger
- 1/2 teaspoon onion powder
- 1/2 teaspoon smoked paprika
- Salt and pepper, to taste

Optional Toppings:

- Pineapple slices
- Red onion slices
- Coleslaw
- Sliced jalapeños

Instructions:

1. Prepare the Hawaiian BBQ Pork:
    - Season the pork shoulder or pork butt with salt and pepper on all sides.
    - In a large skillet or Dutch oven, heat a drizzle of olive oil over medium-high heat. Sear the pork on all sides until browned, about 3-4 minutes per side.
2. Make the Hawaiian BBQ Sauce:
    - In a medium bowl, whisk together all the ingredients for the Hawaiian BBQ sauce until well combined. Set aside.

3. Slow Cook the Pork:
    - Transfer the seared pork to a slow cooker. Add sliced onion, minced garlic, pineapple juice, and low-sodium chicken broth.
    - Pour the Hawaiian BBQ sauce over the pork, ensuring it's well coated.
    - Cover and cook on low for 7-8 hours, or until the pork is tender and easily shreds with a fork.
4. Shred the Pork:
    - Remove the pork from the slow cooker and shred it using two forks. Return the shredded pork to the slow cooker and toss it in the juices and sauce.
5. Assemble the Sliders:
    - Slice the slider buns and lightly toast them if desired.
    - Spoon a generous amount of Hawaiian BBQ pork onto each slider bun.
    - Add optional toppings like pineapple slices, red onion slices, coleslaw, or sliced jalapeños as desired.
6. Serve:
    - Arrange the Hawaiian BBQ pork sliders on a platter and serve warm.

Tips:

- Make-Ahead: The Hawaiian BBQ pork can be prepared ahead of time and stored in an airtight container in the refrigerator for up to 3 days. Reheat gently on the stove or in the microwave before assembling sliders.
- Party Tip: These sliders are perfect for parties or gatherings. Keep the pork warm in a slow cooker or on a low heat setting to allow guests to build their own sliders.
- Variations: Substitute the pork with chicken thighs or beef brisket for different flavors.

Enjoy these Hawaiian BBQ pork sliders for a delicious taste of island-inspired flavors in a convenient and crowd-pleasing format!

Ratatouille

Ingredients:

- 1 large eggplant, diced into 1-inch cubes
- 2 zucchini, diced into 1-inch cubes
- 1 yellow bell pepper, diced
- 1 red bell pepper, diced
- 1 onion, finely chopped
- 4 cloves garlic, minced
- 4 large tomatoes, diced (or 1 can (14 oz) diced tomatoes)
- 2 tablespoons tomato paste
- 1/4 cup olive oil
- 1 teaspoon dried thyme
- 1 teaspoon dried oregano
- 1 bay leaf
- Salt and pepper, to taste
- Fresh basil or parsley, chopped (for garnish)

Instructions:

1. Prepare the Vegetables:
    - Heat 2 tablespoons of olive oil in a large skillet or Dutch oven over medium heat. Add the diced eggplant and sauté for about 5-7 minutes, until lightly browned and softened. Remove from the skillet and set aside.
    - In the same skillet, add another tablespoon of olive oil if needed. Sauté the diced zucchini for about 5 minutes, until slightly softened. Remove and set aside with the eggplant.
    - Add the remaining tablespoon of olive oil to the skillet. Sauté the diced bell peppers and onion for about 5 minutes, until they begin to soften.
2. Cook the Ratatouille:
    - Add the minced garlic to the skillet and cook for 1 minute, until fragrant.
    - Stir in the diced tomatoes, tomato paste, dried thyme, dried oregano, bay leaf, salt, and pepper. Bring to a simmer.
    - Add the sautéed eggplant, zucchini, and bell peppers back into the skillet. Stir gently to combine all the ingredients.
    - Cover and simmer over low heat for about 20-25 minutes, stirring occasionally, until all the vegetables are tender and the flavors have melded together. Adjust seasoning if needed.
3. Serve:
    - Remove the bay leaf from the ratatouille before serving.
    - Garnish with chopped fresh basil or parsley.

Tips:

- Texture: The vegetables should be tender but not mushy. It's important to cook them just until they are softened to maintain their texture.
- Variations: Ratatouille can be served warm, cold, or at room temperature. It can be enjoyed as a side dish, over pasta or rice, or even as a topping for crusty bread.
- Storage: Ratatouille tastes even better the next day as the flavors continue to develop. Store leftovers in an airtight container in the refrigerator for up to 4 days.

Ratatouille is a versatile and comforting dish that highlights the natural flavors of fresh vegetables with Mediterranean herbs. It's perfect for vegetarians and vegans or as a delicious side dish to complement a variety of main courses.

Quiche Lorraine

Ingredients:

For the Pastry Crust:

- 1 1/4 cups all-purpose flour
- 1/2 teaspoon salt
- 1/2 cup unsalted butter, cold and cut into small cubes
- 3-4 tablespoons ice water

For the Filling:

- 6 slices bacon, chopped
- 1/2 cup onion, finely chopped
- 1 cup shredded Gruyere cheese (or Swiss cheese)
- 4 large eggs
- 1 cup heavy cream (or half-and-half)
- Salt and pepper, to taste
- Pinch of nutmeg (optional)
- Fresh parsley, chopped (for garnish)

Instructions:

1. Prepare the Pastry Crust:
    - In a large bowl, whisk together the flour and salt. Add the cold cubed butter.
    - Using a pastry cutter or your fingers, blend the butter into the flour until the mixture resembles coarse crumbs.
    - Gradually add the ice water, one tablespoon at a time, mixing with a fork until the dough comes together and forms a ball.
    - Shape the dough into a disk, wrap it in plastic wrap, and refrigerate for at least 30 minutes.
2. Pre-bake the Crust:
    - Preheat your oven to 375°F (190°C).
    - Roll out the chilled dough on a lightly floured surface to fit a 9-inch tart or pie pan. Press the dough into the pan and trim any excess. Prick the bottom of the crust with a fork.
    - Line the crust with parchment paper or foil and fill with pie weights or dried beans.
    - Bake for 15 minutes. Remove the weights and parchment/foil, then bake for an additional 5 minutes until the crust is golden. Remove from the oven and set aside.
3. Prepare the Filling:

- In a skillet, cook the chopped bacon over medium heat until crispy. Remove bacon from the skillet and drain on paper towels. Reserve 1 tablespoon of bacon fat in the skillet.
- Add chopped onion to the skillet and sauté until softened and translucent, about 5 minutes. Remove from heat and set aside.

4. Assemble and Bake the Quiche:
    - Preheat your oven to 375°F (190°C) again.
    - Sprinkle half of the shredded cheese over the bottom of the pre-baked pastry crust.
    - In a bowl, whisk together the eggs and heavy cream until well combined. Season with salt, pepper, and a pinch of nutmeg if desired.
    - Spread the cooked bacon and sautéed onion evenly over the cheese in the pastry crust.
    - Pour the egg mixture over the bacon and onion. Sprinkle the remaining shredded cheese on top.
5. Bake the Quiche:
    - Place the quiche in the preheated oven and bake for 30-35 minutes, or until the quiche is set and the top is golden brown.
    - Remove from the oven and let it cool for a few minutes before slicing.
    - Garnish with chopped fresh parsley before serving.

Tips:

- **Make-Ahead:** Quiche Lorraine can be assembled and baked up to a day in advance. Let it cool completely, then cover and refrigerate. Reheat in a 325°F (160°C) oven for about 15-20 minutes before serving.
- **Variations:** You can add spinach, mushrooms, or leeks to the filling for different flavors. Adjust the cheese to your preference, using Gruyere, Swiss, or even Cheddar.
- **Serve:** Quiche Lorraine is delicious served warm or at room temperature, making it suitable for brunch, lunch, or a light dinner paired with a salad.

Enjoy this classic Quiche Lorraine with its creamy filling and flaky crust—a timeless dish that never fails to impress!

Teriyaki Beef Skewers

Ingredients:

- 1 lb (450g) beef sirloin or flank steak, cut into 1-inch cubes
- Wooden or metal skewers (if using wooden skewers, soak them in water for 30 minutes before using)
- Sesame seeds, for garnish
- Sliced green onions, for garnish

For the Teriyaki Marinade:

- 1/2 cup soy sauce (low sodium recommended)
- 1/4 cup mirin (Japanese sweet rice wine)
- 1/4 cup water
- 3 tablespoons brown sugar
- 2 cloves garlic, minced
- 1 teaspoon grated ginger
- 1 tablespoon cornstarch mixed with 2 tablespoons water (optional, for thickening)

Instructions:

1. Prepare the Teriyaki Marinade:
    - In a small saucepan, combine soy sauce, mirin, water, brown sugar, minced garlic, and grated ginger. Bring to a simmer over medium heat, stirring occasionally until the sugar is dissolved.
    - If you prefer a thicker sauce, stir in the cornstarch mixture (optional) and simmer for another 1-2 minutes until the sauce thickens slightly. Remove from heat and let it cool to room temperature.
2. Marinate the Beef:
    - Place the beef cubes in a shallow dish or resealable plastic bag. Pour half of the cooled teriyaki marinade over the beef, reserving the other half for basting and serving. Make sure the beef is evenly coated. Cover or seal the bag and refrigerate for at least 1 hour, or ideally overnight for best flavor.
3. Skewer the Beef:
    - Preheat your grill to medium-high heat or preheat your broiler.
    - Thread the marinated beef cubes onto skewers, evenly distributing them with a little space between each piece.
4. Grill or Broil the Skewers:
    - Grill the skewers for about 3-4 minutes per side, or until the beef is cooked to your desired doneness and has nice grill marks. Baste with the reserved teriyaki marinade during grilling.
    - Alternatively, you can broil the skewers in the oven on a broiler pan lined with foil for about 3-4 minutes per side, basting with the marinade.
5. Serve:

- Remove the skewers from the grill or broiler and place them on a serving platter.
- Garnish with sesame seeds and sliced green onions.
- Serve the teriyaki beef skewers hot, with extra teriyaki sauce on the side for dipping or drizzling over rice.

Tips:

- Variations: You can add vegetables such as bell peppers, onions, or mushrooms to the skewers for extra flavor and color.
- Make-Ahead: Marinate the beef ahead of time and store it in the refrigerator until ready to skewer and grill.
- Serve with: Teriyaki beef skewers are delicious served with steamed rice, stir-fried vegetables, or a fresh green salad.

Enjoy these teriyaki beef skewers as a main dish or appetizer for a taste of tender, grilled goodness with a sweet and savory teriyaki glaze!

Coconut Curry Chicken

Ingredients:

For the Chicken Marinade:

- 1 lb (450g) chicken breasts or thighs, cut into bite-sized pieces
- 1 tablespoon curry powder
- 1 teaspoon turmeric powder
- 1 teaspoon ground cumin
- 1 teaspoon paprika
- 1/2 teaspoon salt
- 1/2 teaspoon black pepper
- 2 tablespoons plain yogurt (optional, for tenderness)

For the Curry Sauce:

- 1 tablespoon vegetable oil or coconut oil
- 1 large onion, finely chopped
- 3 cloves garlic, minced
- 1 tablespoon fresh ginger, grated
- 2 tablespoons red curry paste (or yellow/green curry paste for a milder flavor)
- 1 can (14 oz) coconut milk (full-fat or light, based on preference)
- 1 can (14 oz) diced tomatoes (with juice)
- 1 tablespoon tomato paste
- 1 teaspoon brown sugar or honey (optional, for sweetness)
- 1 teaspoon ground coriander
- 1/2 teaspoon ground cumin
- 1/2 teaspoon chili flakes (optional, for heat)
- Salt and pepper, to taste
- Fresh cilantro, chopped (for garnish)
- Cooked rice or naan bread, for serving

Instructions:

1. Marinate the Chicken:
    - In a bowl, mix together the curry powder, turmeric, cumin, paprika, salt, pepper, and yogurt (if using). Add the chicken pieces and coat them well with the marinade. Let it sit for at least 30 minutes, or up to 2 hours in the refrigerator for the flavors to meld.
2. Prepare the Curry Sauce:
    - Heat the vegetable oil or coconut oil in a large skillet or saucepan over medium heat. Add the chopped onion and sauté until it becomes translucent and slightly golden, about 5-7 minutes.

- Add the minced garlic and grated ginger to the onions, and cook for another 1-2 minutes until fragrant.
        - Stir in the red curry paste and cook for 1 minute, allowing the paste to blend with the onions and garlic.
3. Cook the Chicken:
    - Add the marinated chicken pieces to the skillet, stirring well to coat them with the curry paste and onion mixture. Cook for 5-7 minutes, until the chicken is browned on the outside but not fully cooked through.
4. Add Coconut Milk and Tomatoes:
    - Pour in the coconut milk, diced tomatoes (with their juice), tomato paste, brown sugar or honey (if using), ground coriander, ground cumin, and chili flakes (if using). Stir to combine everything well.
    - Bring the mixture to a simmer, then reduce the heat to low. Cover and let it simmer gently for 15-20 minutes, or until the chicken is cooked through and the sauce has thickened slightly. Stir occasionally.
5. Season and Finish:
    - Taste the curry and adjust seasoning with salt and pepper as needed. If you prefer a thicker sauce, you can simmer it uncovered for a few more minutes until it reaches your desired consistency.
6. Serve:
    - Garnish the Coconut Curry Chicken with fresh chopped cilantro.
    - Serve hot over steamed rice or with warm naan bread.

Tips:

- Vegetable Additions: Feel free to add vegetables such as bell peppers, spinach, or peas during the simmering stage for added color and nutrition.
- Make Ahead: This dish tastes even better the next day as the flavors continue to develop. It can be refrigerated for up to 3 days.
- Spice Level: Adjust the amount of curry paste and chili flakes based on your heat preference. For a milder dish, use less curry paste and skip the chili flakes.

Enjoy the creamy, spicy, and aromatic flavors of this Coconut Curry Chicken, a perfect dish to warm you up and satisfy your taste buds!

Grilled Corn on the Cob

Ingredients:

- Fresh corn on the cob, husked
- Butter, softened
- Salt and pepper, to taste
- Optional toppings: chopped fresh herbs (such as parsley or cilantro), grated Parmesan cheese, chili powder, lime wedges

Instructions:

1. Prepare the Corn:
    - Preheat your grill to medium-high heat.
    - Husk the corn and remove the silk. Rinse the corn under cold water and pat dry with paper towels.
2. Grill the Corn:
    - Spread a thin layer of softened butter evenly over each ear of corn. Season with salt and pepper to taste.
    - Place the corn directly on the grill grate. Close the lid and grill for about 10-15 minutes, turning occasionally, until the corn kernels are tender and charred in spots.
3. Serve:
    - Remove the corn from the grill and transfer to a serving platter.
    - Optionally, sprinkle with chopped fresh herbs, grated Parmesan cheese, or a pinch of chili powder for extra flavor. Serve with lime wedges on the side for squeezing over the corn.

Tips:

- Variations: Experiment with different seasonings and toppings such as garlic powder, smoked paprika, or a squeeze of lemon juice.
- Husked Corn: If you prefer to grill corn with the husk on, peel back the husks, remove the silk, and then fold the husks back over the corn before grilling. This method adds a slightly smokier flavor to the corn.
- Grilling Time: The grilling time may vary depending on the heat of your grill and the size of the corn. Keep an eye on the corn and rotate it occasionally to ensure even cooking.

Grilled corn on the cob is a versatile and delightful side dish that pairs perfectly with a variety of main courses, especially during summer gatherings and barbecues. Enjoy the smoky-sweet flavors straight from the grill!

Stuffed Zucchini Boats

Ingredients:

- 4 medium zucchini
- 1 tablespoon olive oil
- 1 small onion, finely chopped
- 2 cloves garlic, minced
- 1 red bell pepper, diced
- 1 cup mushrooms, diced
- 1 teaspoon Italian seasoning (or a mix of dried basil, oregano, and thyme)
- Salt and pepper, to taste
- 1 cup cooked quinoa or rice
- 1/2 cup shredded mozzarella cheese (or any cheese of your choice)
- Fresh parsley or basil, chopped (for garnish)

Instructions:

1. Prepare the Zucchini:
    - Preheat your oven to 400°F (200°C).
    - Cut each zucchini in half lengthwise. Use a spoon to scoop out the flesh from the center of each zucchini half, leaving about 1/4-inch thickness around the edges. Reserve the scooped-out flesh.
2. Prepare the Filling:
    - Heat olive oil in a large skillet over medium heat. Add chopped onion and cook until translucent, about 3-4 minutes.
    - Add minced garlic, diced red bell pepper, and diced mushrooms to the skillet. Cook for another 5-7 minutes, until the vegetables are tender and any liquid has evaporated.
    - Season with Italian seasoning, salt, and pepper. Stir in the reserved zucchini flesh and cook for 2-3 minutes.
3. Assemble the Zucchini Boats:
    - Stir cooked quinoa or rice into the skillet with the vegetable mixture, combining well. Taste and adjust seasoning if needed.
    - Place the hollowed-out zucchini halves on a baking sheet lined with parchment paper or lightly greased.
    - Spoon the filling mixture evenly into each zucchini boat, pressing down gently.
4. Bake the Stuffed Zucchini:
    - Cover the baking sheet with foil and bake in the preheated oven for 20-25 minutes, or until the zucchini is tender.
5. Add Cheese and Finish:
    - Remove the foil from the baking sheet and sprinkle shredded mozzarella cheese evenly over the stuffed zucchini boats.

- Return the baking sheet to the oven and bake for another 5-7 minutes, or until the cheese is melted and bubbly.
6. Serve:
    - Remove from the oven and garnish with chopped fresh parsley or basil.
    - Serve the stuffed zucchini boats warm as a main dish or a side dish.

Tips:

- Variations: Feel free to customize the filling with your favorite ingredients such as ground meat, beans, spinach, or different types of cheese.
- Make-Ahead: You can prepare the filling ahead of time and store it in the refrigerator. Assemble the zucchini boats and bake when ready to serve.
- Vegetarian/Vegan Option: Omit the cheese or use vegan cheese to make this dish vegan-friendly.

Stuffed zucchini boats are a wholesome and satisfying dish that's perfect for a weeknight dinner or as part of a larger meal. Enjoy the blend of flavors and textures in each bite!

Mediterranean Stuffed Pitas

Ingredients:

- 4 whole wheat pita bread rounds
- 1 cup cooked chickpeas (canned or cooked from dry)
- 1 cucumber, diced
- 1 cup cherry tomatoes, halved
- 1/2 red onion, thinly sliced
- 1/2 cup Kalamata olives, pitted and sliced
- 1/2 cup crumbled feta cheese
- Fresh parsley or cilantro, chopped (for garnish)
- Salt and pepper, to taste

For the Greek Yogurt Sauce:

- 1/2 cup Greek yogurt
- 1 tablespoon lemon juice
- 1 tablespoon olive oil
- 1 clove garlic, minced
- 1/2 teaspoon dried dill (or 1 tablespoon fresh dill, chopped)
- Salt and pepper, to taste

Instructions:

1. Prepare the Greek Yogurt Sauce:
   - In a small bowl, whisk together Greek yogurt, lemon juice, olive oil, minced garlic, dried dill (or fresh dill), salt, and pepper. Adjust seasoning to taste. Set aside.
2. Assemble the Stuffed Pitas:
   - Warm the pita bread rounds slightly in the toaster or oven, if desired.
   - Open each pita round to create a pocket.
   - Spread a generous spoonful of Greek yogurt sauce inside each pita pocket.
   - Divide the cooked chickpeas, diced cucumber, halved cherry tomatoes, sliced red onion, Kalamata olives, and crumbled feta cheese evenly among the pitas.
   - Season with salt and pepper to taste.
3. Serve:
   - Garnish the stuffed pitas with chopped fresh parsley or cilantro.
   - Serve immediately, or wrap each pita in foil or parchment paper for an easy grab-and-go meal.

Tips:

- Protein Options: You can add grilled chicken, falafel, or even tofu for added protein.
- Variations: Customize the filling with other Mediterranean ingredients like roasted red peppers, artichoke hearts, or avocado slices.

- Make-Ahead: Prepare the ingredients and Greek yogurt sauce ahead of time, but assemble the pitas just before serving to prevent them from becoming soggy.

These Mediterranean stuffed pitas are refreshing, packed with flavors, and perfect for a quick lunch or dinner option that's both healthy and satisfying. Enjoy the burst of Mediterranean flavors in every bite!

Campfire Nachos

Ingredients:

- 1 bag (10-12 oz) tortilla chips
- 1 cup shredded cheddar cheese
- 1 cup shredded Monterey Jack cheese
- 1 cup cooked and seasoned ground beef or shredded chicken
- 1/2 cup black beans, drained and rinsed
- 1/2 cup corn kernels (fresh, canned, or frozen)
- 1/2 cup diced tomatoes
- 1/4 cup diced red onion
- 1/4 cup sliced black olives
- 1/4 cup pickled jalapeño slices (optional, for heat)
- Fresh cilantro, chopped, for garnish
- Sour cream, guacamole, or salsa, for serving

Instructions:

1. Prepare Your Campfire:
    - Start by building a campfire and allowing it to burn down to hot coals. Alternatively, if using a grill or oven, preheat to 400°F (200°C).
2. Assemble the Nachos:
    - Tear off a large piece of heavy-duty aluminum foil, enough to wrap and create a pouch for the nachos.
    - Spread half of the tortilla chips in an even layer on the aluminum foil.
    - Sprinkle half of the shredded cheddar and Monterey Jack cheese over the chips.
    - Add half of the cooked ground beef or shredded chicken, black beans, corn kernels, diced tomatoes, red onion, black olives, and pickled jalapeño slices (if using).
    - Repeat with another layer of tortilla chips and the remaining toppings.
3. Cook the Nachos:
    - Fold the aluminum foil over the nachos to create a sealed pouch, ensuring all edges are tightly closed to trap steam and heat.
    - Place the foil pouch directly on the hot coals of the campfire or on a grill grate. If using an oven, place the pouch on a baking sheet.
    - Cook for about 10-15 minutes, or until the cheese is melted and bubbly.
4. Serve:
    - Carefully open the foil pouch (watch out for steam) and sprinkle chopped cilantro over the nachos.
    - Serve immediately with sour cream, guacamole, or salsa on the side.

Tips:

- Variations: Customize the toppings based on your preferences. You can add diced bell peppers, cooked bacon, green onions, or different types of cheese.
- Individual Servings: If making individual servings, create smaller foil packets for each person to personalize their nachos.
- Preparation: Prepare all ingredients ahead of time for easy assembly at the campsite or outdoor gathering.

These campfire nachos are a delicious and crowd-pleasing snack or meal that's perfect for sharing around the fire. Enjoy the melted cheese, crispy chips, and flavorful toppings with your favorite outdoor companions!

Chicken and Veggie Foil Packets

Ingredients:

- 4 boneless, skinless chicken breasts
- 2 cups baby potatoes, halved (or quartered if large)
- 1 red bell pepper, sliced
- 1 yellow bell pepper, sliced
- 1 zucchini, sliced
- 1 yellow squash, sliced
- 1 small red onion, thinly sliced
- 4 cloves garlic, minced
- 4 tablespoons olive oil
- 2 tablespoons fresh lemon juice
- 1 teaspoon dried oregano
- 1 teaspoon dried thyme
- Salt and pepper, to taste
- Fresh herbs (such as parsley or basil), chopped for garnish

Instructions:

1. Preheat the Grill or Oven:
   - Preheat your grill to medium-high heat or preheat your oven to 400°F (200°C).
2. Prepare Foil Packets:
   - Tear off 4 large pieces of heavy-duty aluminum foil, about 12x12 inches each.
   - Place one chicken breast in the center of each piece of foil.
3. Prepare Veggies:
   - In a large bowl, combine baby potatoes, sliced bell peppers, zucchini, yellow squash, red onion, and minced garlic.
   - Drizzle olive oil and lemon juice over the vegetables. Sprinkle with dried oregano, dried thyme, salt, and pepper. Toss to coat evenly.
4. Assemble Foil Packets:
   - Divide the vegetable mixture evenly among the foil packets, arranging them around each chicken breast.
   - Drizzle any remaining olive oil and lemon juice mixture over the chicken and vegetables.
5. Seal Foil Packets:
   - Fold the sides of the foil over the chicken and vegetables, sealing the edges tightly to create a packet. Leave a little room for steam to circulate inside.
6. Cook Foil Packets:
   - Place the foil packets directly on the preheated grill or on a baking sheet in the oven.
   - Grill or bake for 20-25 minutes, or until the chicken is cooked through (internal temperature of 165°F or 75°C) and the vegetables are tender.

7. Serve:
    - Carefully open the foil packets (watch out for steam) and transfer the contents to plates.
    - Garnish with chopped fresh herbs, such as parsley or basil, before serving.

Tips:

- Variations: You can customize the veggies based on what you have on hand or your preferences. Try adding cherry tomatoes, mushrooms, asparagus, or broccoli.
- Marinade: For extra flavor, marinate the chicken in a mixture of olive oil, lemon juice, garlic, and herbs for 30 minutes to overnight before assembling the foil packets.
- Individual Packets: If serving a group with different preferences, create individual foil packets with customized ingredients.

These chicken and veggie foil packets are not only easy to make but also allow for easy cleanup—perfect for busy weeknights or outdoor gatherings. Enjoy the juicy chicken and tender vegetables seasoned with herbs and lemon!

Thai Peanut Noodles

Ingredients:

- 8 oz (225g) rice noodles or linguine noodles
- 1/3 cup creamy peanut butter
- 1/4 cup soy sauce (or tamari for gluten-free)
- 2 tablespoons rice vinegar
- 2 tablespoons lime juice
- 2 tablespoons honey or maple syrup
- 1 tablespoon sesame oil
- 1 tablespoon fresh ginger, grated
- 2 cloves garlic, minced
- 1/4 teaspoon red pepper flakes (adjust to taste)
- 1/3 cup warm water (or more as needed for desired consistency)
- 1 cup shredded carrots
- 1 cup thinly sliced bell peppers (red, yellow, or orange)
- 1/2 cup chopped green onions
- 1/4 cup chopped fresh cilantro
- Optional garnishes: chopped peanuts, sesame seeds, lime wedges

Instructions:

1. Cook the Noodles:
    - Cook the rice noodles according to package instructions until al dente. Drain and rinse with cold water to stop the cooking process. Set aside.
2. Make the Peanut Sauce:
    - In a medium bowl, whisk together peanut butter, soy sauce, rice vinegar, lime juice, honey or maple syrup, sesame oil, grated ginger, minced garlic, and red pepper flakes until smooth.
    - Gradually whisk in warm water, a little at a time, until the sauce reaches your desired consistency. The sauce should be creamy and pourable. Set aside.
3. Assemble the Dish:
    - In a large mixing bowl, toss the cooked noodles with the shredded carrots, sliced bell peppers, and chopped green onions.
    - Pour the peanut sauce over the noodles and vegetables. Toss until everything is well coated in the sauce.
4. Serve:
    - Divide the Thai peanut noodles among serving bowls.
    - Garnish with chopped fresh cilantro, chopped peanuts or sesame seeds, and a lime wedge.
    - Serve immediately and enjoy!

Tips:

- Protein Additions: You can add cooked chicken, shrimp, tofu, or edamame for added protein.
- Adjust Spiciness: Increase or decrease the amount of red pepper flakes according to your preference for spiciness.
- Make-Ahead: Prepare the peanut sauce and cook the noodles in advance. Toss together just before serving for best texture.

Thai peanut noodles are a versatile dish that can be enjoyed warm or cold, making them perfect for lunch, dinner, or as a side dish for gatherings. The combination of creamy peanut sauce and fresh vegetables creates a delightful harmony of flavors and textures.

Grilled Sausage with Peppers and Onions

Ingredients:

- 4 Italian sausages (sweet or hot), or your favorite type
- 2 bell peppers (red, yellow, or green), sliced
- 1 large onion, sliced
- 2 tablespoons olive oil
- 2 cloves garlic, minced
- 1 teaspoon dried Italian seasoning (or a mix of dried basil, oregano, and thyme)
- Salt and pepper, to taste
- Fresh parsley or basil, chopped, for garnish
- Crusty bread or rolls, for serving (optional)

Instructions:

1. Prepare the Grill:
   - Preheat your grill to medium-high heat.
2. Prepare the Sausages:
   - Brush the sausages lightly with olive oil to prevent sticking on the grill.
3. Grill the Sausages:
   - Place the sausages on the preheated grill. Grill for about 15-20 minutes, turning occasionally, until fully cooked through and nicely browned on all sides. The internal temperature should reach 160°F (70°C).
4. Prepare the Peppers and Onions:
   - While the sausages are grilling, heat 2 tablespoons of olive oil in a large skillet over medium heat.
   - Add the sliced bell peppers and onions to the skillet. Cook, stirring occasionally, until the vegetables are softened and lightly caramelized, about 10-12 minutes.
   - Stir in minced garlic and dried Italian seasoning. Season with salt and pepper to taste. Cook for another 1-2 minutes until the garlic is fragrant.
5. Combine and Serve:
   - Once the sausages are cooked through, transfer them to a cutting board and let them rest for a few minutes.
   - Slice the sausages diagonally into bite-sized pieces.
   - Add the sliced sausages to the skillet with the peppers and onions. Toss everything together to combine.
6. Serve:
   - Transfer the grilled sausage, peppers, and onions to a serving platter.
   - Garnish with chopped fresh parsley or basil.
   - Serve hot, either on its own or with crusty bread or rolls for making sandwiches.

Tips:

- Variations: Use different types of sausages such as bratwurst, chorizo, or chicken sausage for variety.
- Make-Ahead: You can precook the sausages and vegetables earlier in the day and quickly reheat them on the grill or stovetop before serving.
- Side Suggestions: Serve with a side of mustard, hot sauce, or a dollop of pesto for extra flavor.

Grilled sausage with peppers and onions is a flavorful and satisfying dish that's perfect for summer cookouts or any casual gathering. Enjoy the smoky flavors of the grilled sausages paired with the sweetness of the caramelized peppers and onions!

Mediterranean Chicken Pita Pockets

Ingredients:

- 1 lb (450g) boneless, skinless chicken breasts, thinly sliced
- 2 tablespoons olive oil
- 2 cloves garlic, minced
- 1 teaspoon dried oregano
- 1 teaspoon dried thyme
- Salt and pepper, to taste
- 4 whole wheat pita bread rounds
- 1 cup cherry tomatoes, halved
- 1 cucumber, thinly sliced
- 1/2 red onion, thinly sliced
- 1/2 cup Kalamata olives, pitted and sliced
- 1/2 cup crumbled feta cheese
- Fresh parsley or basil, chopped, for garnish
- Optional: Tzatziki sauce or hummus for serving

Instructions:

1. Marinate and Cook the Chicken:
    - In a bowl, combine olive oil, minced garlic, dried oregano, dried thyme, salt, and pepper. Add the sliced chicken breasts and toss to coat evenly. Let marinate for at least 15-20 minutes.
    - Heat a grill pan or skillet over medium-high heat. Cook the marinated chicken slices for about 5-7 minutes per side, or until fully cooked and nicely browned. Remove from heat and let rest for a few minutes. Slice into strips.
2. Prepare the Pita Pockets:
    - Warm the pita bread rounds in the microwave or oven to make them more pliable.
    - Open each pita round to create a pocket.
3. Assemble the Pita Pockets:
    - Divide the cooked chicken strips among the pita pockets.
    - Stuff each pita pocket with cherry tomatoes, cucumber slices, red onion slices, Kalamata olives, and crumbled feta cheese.
4. Serve:
    - Garnish the pita pockets with chopped fresh parsley or basil.
    - Optionally, drizzle with tzatziki sauce or spread hummus inside the pita pockets before stuffing.
    - Serve immediately and enjoy!

Tips:

- Variations: Add roasted red peppers, artichoke hearts, or fresh spinach leaves for additional Mediterranean flavors.
- Make-Ahead: Prepare the chicken and vegetables ahead of time, but assemble the pita pockets just before serving to keep them fresh and avoid sogginess.
- Side Suggestions: Serve with a side salad, Greek salad, or roasted vegetables for a complete meal.

These Mediterranean chicken pita pockets are perfect for a quick and flavorful lunch or dinner. They're portable, versatile, and packed with fresh ingredients that capture the essence of Mediterranean cuisine. Enjoy the combination of tender chicken, crisp vegetables, and creamy feta cheese all wrapped in warm pita bread!

Veggie Spring Rolls

Ingredients:

- 8-10 spring roll rice paper wrappers
- 1 cup shredded lettuce or cabbage
- 1 cup shredded carrots
- 1 cucumber, julienned
- 1 bell pepper (red, yellow, or green), julienned
- 1 avocado, sliced (optional)
- 1/2 cup fresh herbs (such as mint, basil, or cilantro), chopped
- Rice vermicelli noodles, cooked according to package instructions (optional)
- Soy sauce or tamari, for dipping (optional)

Instructions:

1. Prepare the Fillings:
    - Prepare all your vegetables by shredding or julienning them into thin strips. You can also cook rice vermicelli noodles according to package instructions if using.
2. Soften the Rice Paper Wrappers:
    - Fill a shallow dish with warm water.
    - Dip one rice paper wrapper into the warm water for about 5-10 seconds until it becomes soft and pliable.
    - Place the softened rice paper wrapper on a clean, damp kitchen towel or cutting board.
3. Assemble the Spring Rolls:
    - Layer a small amount of each filling ingredient (lettuce or cabbage, carrots, cucumber, bell pepper, avocado if using, herbs, and noodles if using) in the center of the rice paper wrapper.
    - Fold the sides of the rice paper wrapper over the filling. Then, gently fold the bottom of the wrapper over the filling and roll tightly.
    - Continue rolling until the spring roll is sealed. Place seam-side down on a serving plate.
4. Repeat:
    - Repeat with the remaining rice paper wrappers and filling ingredients until all the fillings are used.
5. Serve:
    - Serve the veggie spring rolls whole, or cut in half diagonally.
    - Serve with soy sauce or tamari for dipping, if desired.

Tips:

- Variations: You can add cooked shrimp, tofu, or vermicelli noodles to the filling for added protein.

- Storage: Spring rolls are best served fresh but can be stored in an airtight container in the refrigerator for up to a day. If storing, separate layers with parchment paper to prevent sticking.
- Dipping Sauces: Besides soy sauce or tamari, you can serve with peanut sauce, hoisin sauce mixed with a bit of sriracha for spice, or a sweet chili sauce.

These veggie spring rolls are light, refreshing, and perfect for a healthy appetizer, snack, or light meal. Enjoy the combination of crunchy vegetables and herbs wrapped in delicate rice paper!

Campfire Potatoes

Ingredients:

- 4-6 medium potatoes (such as Russet or Yukon Gold), washed and thinly sliced
- 1 onion, thinly sliced
- 2-3 cloves garlic, minced
- 2 tablespoons olive oil or melted butter
- Salt and pepper, to taste
- Optional seasonings: paprika, garlic powder, dried herbs (such as thyme or rosemary)
- Heavy-duty aluminum foil

Instructions:

1. Prepare the Campfire:
   - Build a campfire and allow it to burn down to hot coals. Alternatively, if grilling, preheat your grill to medium-high heat.
2. Prepare Foil Packets:
   - Tear off 4 large pieces of heavy-duty aluminum foil, about 12x12 inches each.
3. Assemble the Potatoes:
   - In a large bowl, toss together thinly sliced potatoes, sliced onion, minced garlic, olive oil or melted butter, salt, pepper, and any optional seasonings you like.
4. Divide and Wrap:
   - Divide the potato mixture evenly among the foil pieces, placing it in the center.
   - Fold the sides of the foil over the potatoes, sealing the edges tightly to create a packet. Leave a little room for steam to circulate inside.
5. Cook Over the Campfire:
   - Place the foil packets directly on the hot coals of the campfire or on the preheated grill grate.
   - Cook for about 20-25 minutes, flipping once halfway through, or until the potatoes are tender when pierced with a fork.
6. Serve:
   - Carefully open the foil packets (watch out for steam) and transfer the cooked campfire potatoes to a serving dish.
   - Serve hot as a delicious side dish for your outdoor meal.

Tips:

- Variations: Add other vegetables like bell peppers or mushrooms to the foil packets for added flavor and variety.
- Cheesy Option: Sprinkle shredded cheese over the potatoes during the last few minutes of cooking for cheesy campfire potatoes.
- Herb Butter: Use herb-infused butter (such as garlic herb butter) instead of plain olive oil or butter for extra flavor.

Campfire potatoes are a simple yet flavorful way to enjoy the outdoors while cooking. They pair well with grilled meats, fish, or as part of a vegetarian meal. Enjoy the smoky aroma and tender, seasoned potatoes straight from the fire!

S'mores Dip

Ingredients:

- 1 cup milk chocolate chips (or chopped chocolate)
- 1 cup mini marshmallows
- 1/4 cup heavy cream (or milk)
- Graham crackers, for serving

Instructions:

1. Preheat the Oven:
   - Preheat your oven to 350°F (175°C).
2. Prepare the Baking Dish:
   - Lightly grease a small oven-safe dish or skillet (about 6-8 inches in diameter).
3. Assemble the Dip:
   - Spread the milk chocolate chips evenly in the bottom of the greased dish.
   - Top with mini marshmallows, spreading them evenly over the chocolate chips.
4. Bake the Dip:
   - Pour the heavy cream (or milk) evenly over the chocolate and marshmallows.
   - Place the dish in the preheated oven and bake for about 10-15 minutes, or until the marshmallows are golden brown and gooey, and the chocolate is melted and bubbly.
5. Serve:
   - Remove from the oven and let it cool slightly.
   - Serve the s'mores dip warm, with graham crackers for dipping.

Tips:

- Variations: You can use different types of chocolate (dark chocolate, white chocolate) or add toppings like crushed nuts, caramel sauce, or even peanut butter for a different twist.
- Broil Option: For a quicker golden brown on top, broil the dip for the last 1-2 minutes, but watch carefully to avoid burning the marshmallows.
- Microwave Option: If you prefer, you can assemble the dip in a microwave-safe dish and microwave in short bursts until the chocolate is melted and marshmallows are puffed and golden.

S'mores dip is a fun and easy dessert that brings the flavors of traditional s'mores indoors. It's perfect for parties, family gatherings, or a cozy night in. Enjoy the gooey, chocolatey goodness with the crunch of graham crackers!

www.ingramcontent.com/pod-product-compliance
Lightning Source LLC
LaVergne TN
LVHW062047070526
838201LV00080B/2163